56 New Income Streams for Financial Advisers

PHILIP CALVERT

56 New Income Streams for Financial Advisers

How to Turn your Financial Planning Expertise & Experience into Profitable New Products and Services for the Digital Age

Philip Calvert

Copyright © 2019 Philip Calvert

All rights reserved. This book or any portion thereof may not be reproduced or used in any manner whatsoever without the express written permission of the publisher except for the use of brief quotations in a book review or scholarly journal.

First Printing: 2019

ISBN: 978-1-68-912981-7

PHILIP CALVERT

This book is dedicated to the thousands of financial advisers I have met whilst speaking at conferences and events over a forty-year career. Times are changing for the financial advice profession, and I hope that you will find this book to be a valuable resource as you look to the future.

Contents

Acknowledgements

Introduction

Seminars

Bootcamps

Client Retreats

Seminar Recordings

Seminar Transcripts

Public Speaking

Schools

Webinars

Workbooks and Handouts

Tips Booklets

eBooks

Audio Books

Physical Books (Published)

Physical Books (Self-Published)

Case Study Books

'Diary of a…' Books

Co-Authored Books

Mini-Books

Special Reports and White Papers

Courses

Membership Sites and Online Communities

Networking Groups and Meetings

Executive and Peer-to-Peer Mastermind Groups

Conferences and Online Summits

Software and Apps

Thirty-four Additional Ideas

Your Value Ladder Revisited

Going Up a Gear

Your Challenge

Next Steps

Progressing the Relationship

Building Relationships through Online Groups

Final Tips

About the Author

Disclaimer and Terms of Use

Acknowledgements

It's impossible to acknowledge everyone who has given me help and inspiration during the development of this project. Suffice to say that I continue to be inspired every day by the creativity of information marketers around the world, and the opportunities for personal growth they bring to people everywhere.

PHILIP CALVERT

Introduction

Every year I personally meet hundreds of financial advisers and speak to thousands more at conferences and events where I am presenting or training.

On one day alone last year, I spoke to four thousand financial advisers at a conference in Johannesburg and went on to personally meet hundreds at a networking event later in the evening.

Since I started working with financial advisers in 1978, there has been one consistent topic that is raised time and time again in conversations, at conferences, seminars, industry publications, training events and in online forums – how to generate (quality) leads.

And to be clear, these are leads over and above those that naturally come in from referrals; with referrals generally said to be the main source of leads for financial advisers.

But the fact that the question of how to generate leads comes up so often, and at all levels within the financial advice community, suggests that many financial advisers are not receiving as many (quality) referrals as they would wish. Referral generation is a valuable skill and strategy in its own right, which is outside the scope of this book, so in due course I will highlight a fantastic resource that will supercharge the number and quality of your referrals. You'll thank me later.

In the meantime, 'repackaging your expertise' as a financial adviser is without doubt, one of the best ways to generate leads.

By 'repackaging' we mean creating new products and services from your expertise, experience, knowledge and skills as an adviser.

This is important because most IFAs and financial advisers regard their sole service as financial planning or financial advice – an activity that has traditionally only been conducted between consenting adults in either the client's home or the adviser's office. But your proposition need not (and arguably *should not*) just be restricted to financial planning, review meetings and related peripheral services.

Thanks to today's technology, it is possible to break down financial planning and advice into smaller user-friendly products which have a variety of benefits to you and your clients.

Creating new products and services from your expertise has a number of benefits:

- They create 'Lead Magnets' to make your website more engaging

- They give people a sneak peek into your skills and expertise before committing to a full financial planning exercise

- The creation of a clear 'Value Ladder' for advisers

- New ways to add value to people who cannot afford to pay for full financial planning

- New ways for people to get financial information without having to meet an adviser

- Enhancement of the perception of your expertise as an adviser

- A route to transitioning away from the regulated environment

- A valuable new income stream for advisers

Financial planning, or elements of it can be given or sold to clients in many different ways, formats and mediums, and that's what this book is looking at in more detail.

Many of the approaches I'm going to describe are very powerful ways to generate leads for your financial advice business, and that's great – but what I'm more interested in is how they can also create an income stream in their own right.

Just imagine, a marketing technique which attracts high quality clients – *and* which also brings in its own income…

First up is Seminars.

Seminars

Whilst I'm the first person to say that financial advisers should be embracing the digital world very much more than they currently do, I'm also the first person to say that seminars are, in my view, the single most effective way for advisers to generate quality new leads.

The majority of the most successful advisers around the world, use or have used seminars and client events as part of their marketing at some stage.

Why? Because they work.

Seminars are about building trust with potential prospects. They give people the opportunity to see the whites of your eyes and to 'try before they buy'.

The concept of Financial Planning has been very poorly marketed by the profession over many years, but that's largely because it's one of those products or services that needs to be *seen and experienced* before people really understand it.

That's one of the reasons why Financial Life Planners often receive referrals after the very first meeting with a client. The experience is often so powerful that they cannot help but refer the adviser to their friends. An experience that is particularly difficult to express on a website.

Hosting a local seminar gives people the opportunity to experience an adviser's expertise - and usually in an attractive, friendly and professional environment.

But the best part is that when done properly, seminars have astonishingly high conversion rates. I know several advisers who regularly see conversion rates at their seminars in excess of 80%. 100% is not uncommon.

So that's how you can use seminars as a lead generator – but what about using them to create an income stream in their own right…

The majority of adviser's seminars are free to attend, but increasingly they are chargeable. In fact, this has been the case for many years throughout the USA. And it makes good sense.

I know of an adviser in the UK, who for three years would run a local seminar every quarter. The objectives for his seminars were:

- To raise his profile in the area

- To build closer relationships with local professional connections

- To build relationships with local press

- To add value to *existing* clients, and

- To attract quality *new* clients.

His conversion rates were 90%+ and they were working well. Typically, he would have fifty people in the room every time.

After three years of doing this, his business adviser suggested that he charge for his seminars. Fearful that this would put off people from attending, he reluctantly agreed to charge approximately £90 for attendance, including a quality wine tasting for every attendee.

To his amazement, *more* people wanted to attend than when the event was free. What's more, the perception of value was such that 'higher quality people' turned up.

Now let's do some multiplication:

50 (people) x £90 = £4,500

£4,500 x 4 (events per year) = £18,000

Think that's good?

Over in the US - businessman, philanthropist and author Nido Qubein runs a 'Wealth Weekend' where he shows his delegates:

"...how to make money, save it, invest it, fertilize it, protect it and use it to build congruent ventures and fulfilling stewardship that helps others – plus how to align your planning with practical and impactful action plans".

The cost of a ticket is $12,600.

With numbers like these, it's no wonder that many financial advisers around the world are now pulling back from the regulated environment and starting to transition from selling financial advice and planning, to selling financial information. Where someone does want face to face advice after an event, this is done by a regulated adviser within the advice firm or passed on to someone else.

And this is just the start of the income possibilities from hosting seminars and events. Charging for attendance can be combined with some of the other tactics I'm about to share, which boosts your income even further.

And remember, seminars are primarily used as a proven way to generate leads. Now you have a tactic which not only brings in new clients, but one where they pay to be prospects.

Before we end this section, it's also worth saying that simply *promoting* a seminar can be enough to attract clients. Martin Bamford at Informed Choice Independent Financial Planning has told me that on more than one occasion he has attracted new clients who had never heard of him until they saw his promotions for his local seminars. They couldn't actually make the date of the seminar, but it was enough for them to decide to contact Informed Choice.

For now, we don't need to go into the practicalities of planning, promoting and presenting your seminar because I'll point you to a resource later in this book. But it's worth bearing mind that there are various permutations on the seminar theme, so let's look at the next logical steps from seminars and workshops – Bootcamps and Client Retreats.

Bootcamps

Just imagine a seminar but a bit more hardcore! It is less of the nice presentational approach and more hands on with in-depth content, practical exercises and at a deeper technical level.

There are various models for this type of event, but the important thing is that a one size does not fit all. Bootcamps tend to be well targeted, with a focus on a niche market – for example:

- Lawyers nearing retirement
- Financial Planning for surgeons
- Retirement Planning for CEOs of mid-sized companies
- Investing for tech entrepreneurs
- Etc.

The format of the event will typically be over two days and will follow the full financial planning process for (say) lawyers nearing retirement in depth. Attendees will need to be willing to share details of their personal circumstances, and happy to undergo live financial planning in front of other attendees – often using cashflow modelling tools projected on a screen.

As you can imagine, attendance will usually be fewer than ten people and the event will be high quality in a great venue. Quite apart from the content of the event, attendees will find the networking hugely valuable.

The more niche market you can make your event, the better – and you can also expect excellent referrals from others within that niche.

It's not for every adviser, but there will be many who'll love this fresh and in-depth approach.

One final point – think carefully about what you call such an event. For example, will lawyers nearing retirement be attracted to the idea of a Financial Planning "Bootcamp"? Choose a title that is appropriate to your market and target audience for your event.

Client Retreats

A seminar is a proven and highly effective way to attract new clients – and one that can monetised. Many of the advisers who are successful at hosting seminars make a point of inviting existing clients to their events. This is because although they are already clients, inviting them to attend is a great way to keep the relationship plates spinning beyond just review meetings.

Inviting them to attend your seminar also reminds them of your services, and invariably they will refer someone to you after your event. One set of figures I saw a while ago said that when any of us attend an event that we enjoy, we will tell six other people about it. And this was before social media came along. You only have to glance at Facebook to see people regularly sharing photos and videos of an event they are attending to hundreds if not thousands of people.

So how can we take our existing clients further up our Value Ladder – beyond the full financial planning services that we already provide them with?

The answer is a Client Retreat. Imagine a normal client seminar, but at a completely different level of quality.

Usually a client retreat will be a long weekend event held at a luxury location – very often overseas. By definition, such an event will be expensive. It will be out of the reach of most of your clients, but to others it will be hugely compelling, or at the very least something to be aspired to.

We are only limited by our own imaginations as to what can be included in our retreat, but typically it will be very high value, set in a glorious hotel or location, may include specialist expert speakers on a range of topics (not purely financial related), will include excursions, activities and of course great food.

It should not be pitched as a client 'reward' or thank you. This is something that is part of your business proposition and sits at the very top of your Value Ladder. It gives you and a select group of your clients the opportunity to build even closer relationships, and the chance to meet each other in an exclusive environment.

Personal development guru Tony Robbins offers several training experiences on his Value Ladder, starting with free videos on YouTube, rising through a variety of live events of increasing value and expense – culminating with his Platinum Partnership experience at approx. $85,000 per year.

Here's how it is described on his website:

"The Tony Robbins Platinum Partnership is an exclusive opportunity designed for those committed to living life at a level few may ever attain. The Platinum Partnership provides the unprecedented opportunity to network with and learn from Tony and master teachers from around the world, while traveling to the most spectacular destinations on earth."

I understand that there is a little-known even higher level where those with the aspiration to do so can spend significantly higher amounts to spend time with Tony and a select group at his home.

Fish where the Fish are…

Jared Reynolds is a financial planner based in Columbia, Missouri whose niche market is people who enjoy bass fishing and other outdoor pursuits.

Jared arranges a range of retreats and events specifically targeted at these clients. And to be clear, these are all chargeable events which the clients pay for, and which ultimately take his relationships with them to a completely different level.

In short, regardless of your client type, there will be a small group who will willingly invest in a quality event hosted by you and your business. It doesn't necessarily have to be held at an exclusive overseas location – it can simply be something that you feel would be appealing and of value to a select group of your clients.

Retreats should not be confused with Bootcamps. Yes, both are expensive and high quality, but different in the content presented.

And if you want to be fancy, our friend Nido Qubein mentioned earlier runs an event which is a cross between a Retreat and a Bootcamp, which he calls a 'Symposium'.

Seminar Recordings

Whilst you're hosting your seminars, you should record them either on audio or video (or both).

Firstly, you could give the recordings away to your attendees as a thank you gift, or as a means to help them remember the content afterwards - but a better option is to offer the recording as an upsell when booking attendance at the seminar itself.

In my own experience, you will often find that up to fifty percent of the people who pay to attend the event itself, will also be willing to pay an additional amount for a video or audio recording.

Or, you make your seminar free but on the booking page they can choose to pay for a recording which they will receive shortly afterwards.

As another alternative, where you have hosted a free event, people will often be keen to pay for a CD/DVD copy of a previous event, and you can sell these at the back of the room. I've seen several IFAs do this very well. Today you might provide the recordings on a branded memory stick.

Finally, don't forget that attendees of your Bootcamp would also more than likely want a video or audio recording of the event, but here you should bundle the recording into the cost of attending the Bootcamp – thus increasing the perceived value.

When promoting chargeable events, particularly high value events, it's vital that potential attendees can clearly see that there is indeed value. The event itself clearly *is* high value, but you also need to include a variety of other valuable 'bonuses for attendance'. These could be other products and services that you offer such as:

- Your book (Value £20)
- Your online course (Value £496)
- Your Special Report on XYZ topic (Value £1,200)
- Audio and video recording of the event (Value £95)
- Membership of your private networking group (Value £700)
- Overnight accommodation
- Use of the spa
- Etc.

These are just examples of bonuses for attendance, but you should always come up with a few items along these lines.

You should also state the value of each item so that your prospect attendee can see that your bonuses have actual monetary value. At a subconscious level they are thinking that if you are prepared to include all this additional value for attending your event, then the content of the event itself will most likely also be high.

This is a technique known as 'stacking' and used by most of the world's best internet marketers and seminar and event hosts. When I started out giving seminars to financial advisers in the 1980s, I very quickly learnt the power of the bacon roll in my stack!

Seminar Transcriptions

Again, if you have an audio or video recording of a previous event, you can transcribe it and sell it as such – either on your website or at a future event.

Unless you have someone who is happy to transcribe your recording, there are several high quality and inexpensive services on the internet. I use Temi and Rev which are both excellent.

But as you'll see later in this book, transcriptions of events and meetings are proving very popular at the moment. They tick all the right boxes in a modern financial advice business as:

- A powerful lead magnet on your website
- A product that you can create and sell in its own right
- A product that can act as an upsell after purchasing something else
- A gift for attendance at an event
- A product that people can purchase at your event
- A product that can be included in your stack of bonuses for attending an event
- An item that enhances the perception of your expertise

And although your transcription is a 'repurposing' of your seminar, it could also be the basis of perhaps a training course or podcast that you could create in the future.

Public Speaking

If you are hosting a seminar or client event, at some point you will need to get on your feet and give a presentation – even if it's just to welcome guests.

But what about considering adding professional speaking to your proposition?

I know several people within the financial advice world and wider financial services industry who have not only added speaking to their proposition but have made it their career.

Financial Services 'veterans' Frank Furness and Rikki Arundel are now full time global professional speakers, with other advisers such as Bhupinder Anand spending a significant proportion of their time speaking around the world.

You may also have heard of Allan Pease from Australia. He started out in Life Assurance sales and is now one of the world's leading speakers on body language and relationships. He and his wife Barbara have written eighteen bestsellers – including ten number ones – and given seminars in seventy countries. Their books are bestsellers in over one hundred countries, are translated into fifty-five languages and have sold over twenty-seven million copies.

More recent additions to the speaking world from the UK financial planning sector include Jason Butler (formerly of Bloomsbury) and Michelle Hoskin. There are many more who are getting invitations to speak at a range of local and international events.

And they are not just Financial Services events… Conference organisers are increasingly looking for experts on personal finance and life planning in a range of different industries.

Is there really a demand for Speakers on Personal Finance?

Quite apart from many people's natural reticence to speak in public, I have had a number of financial advisers ask me if people really want to hear speakers on the subject of personal finance. Is there actually any demand?

In many respects this question gets to the heart of what I'm trying to do with this book – that is to take personal finance knowledge, expertise and experience, and repackage it into new formats. Formats which for many people are far more convenient and attractive than the traditional ways that they access help and information on the subject.

Let's take just one outlet for speakers on personal finance – TED conferences.

According to the official TED website, there are six talks where the topic includes or covers personal finance:

- Elizabeth White: An honest look at the personal finance crisis
- John Doerr: Why the secret to success is setting the right goals
- Tammy Lally: Let's get honest about our money problems

- Keith Chen: Could your language affect your ability to save money
- Curtis "Wall Street" Carroll: How I learned to read – and trade stocks – in prison
- Tim Ferriss: Why you should define your fears instead of your goals

Just six videos, but between them they have a total of twenty-two million views.

There are a further twenty-two videos which are included under the topics of Getting Paid What You Are Worth, How To Invest In Social Good and Emerging Markets – again with total views around thirty-eight million.

And these exclude many more presentations made at the popular TEDx events.

A quick Google video search for 'Personal Finance' reveals one hundred and forty-four million results.

'Retirement Planning' produces over six million video results.

'Pension Planning' produces four hundred thousand video results.

'Learn Investing' produces over eleven million video results.

'Life Insurance' produces seventy-nine million video results.

And so on…

There's absolutely no reason why any financial adviser can't join this party, and it's great to see our UK based financial planning friend Pete Matthew of MeaningfulMoney with four hundred videos of his own on his YouTube channel.

There are many great books and resources on how to earn from public speaking – plus the art and business of speaking, so I won't go into details here – but I would recommend you look at joining Toastmasters or the Professional Speaking Association (PSA) where you will learn a lot about this amazing industry.

Another great resource is my own online coaching group SpeakerCom which includes a group for Financial Services speakers. Join at https://speaking-professionals.mn.co

Schools

A good way into speaking professionally is to speak in schools. Personal finance education is becoming more important at younger ages and many schools invite speakers in to speak to students. There are even dedicated speaker bureaus that only specialise in speakers for schools and there are people who specialise in coaching school speakers.

Don't expect to always get paid a fee by schools. In many countries, budgets for speakers are very low down the priority list but it is always worth asking if they have a budget because they can often find it somewhere. Certainly in the UK, private schools will have budgets for a wide variety of visiting speakers.

Either way, a good route into a school is to look up their Careers Lead and make contact that way. Schools often run careers weeks where they invite in local businesspeople and also inspirational speakers. Outside that, schools will put on special events with an outside speaker, so again if you have a great message and story to tell, that could get you in front of hundreds, if not thousands of students.

I do a presentation for thirteen to eighteen-year olds on how to use LinkedIn as part of their career planning and I give each student a short leaflet of LinkedIn tips, which on several occasions has resulted in a parent asking me for help.

Don't forget too that universities often have visiting speakers, and I've been lucky enough to speak at the University of Cambridge.

Even if you don't get paid, speaking in schools is incredibly rewarding. And do bear in mind that parents often take an interest in who is speaking in their children's school, and I have known IFAs to attract new clients simply because a student went home and told their folks about it.

Looking for personal coaching on presenting and speaking? Contact me at philip@philipcalvert.com for further information.

Webinars

Just like seminars, webinars can be a powerful way to attract new clients. Yet hardly any financial advisers use them in their marketing mix, let alone as a standalone revenue builder.

There are generally eight approaches you can take for your webinar:

1. Free to attend and presented live online without a promotional element. i.e. pure value

2. Free and presented live online with a promotional element

3. Chargeable and presented live without a promotional element

4. Chargeable and presented live with a promotional element

5. Free recording of a previous webinar without a promotional element

6. Free recording of a previous webinar with a promotional element

7. Chargeable recording of a previous webinar without a promotional element

8. Chargeable recording of a previous webinar with a promotional element

Each model has its place and depends entirely on what you are trying to achieve or where it sits on your Value Ladder. However, audiences in different countries have different attitudes to webinars in general depending on the industry.

Most webinar hosts opt for the 'free plus promotion' approach, either live or recorded. The thinking being that you spend approximately an hour providing very high value, followed by a further thirty to sixty minutes offering a promotion which invariable sells the implementation solution.

When done well and professionally, this approach can be remarkably effective and can bring in very large amounts of revenue. However, this approach is not ideal in the financial advice space, and many financial planners (particularly in the UK) struggle to see how this can work for them. But there is definitely a place for this model when thought-through carefully.

In fact, just like 'real' seminars, there is a system for presenting webinars – a proven approach which just works. Again, we don't have time to go into this in detail here, but contact me at philip@philipcalvert.com for a fantastic resource on this.

For most financial advisers, the best options to go for with webinars are one of the following:

1. Free and presented live online without a promotional element. i.e. pure value

2. Chargeable and presented live without a promotional element

3. Free recording of a previous webinar without a promotional element

4. Chargeable recording of a previous webinar without a promotional element

In summary, offer free webinars to attract new clients and to add value to existing clients, or offer chargeable webinars without a promotional element as a revenue generator.

Workbooks and Handouts

Whether you run seminars or webinars, you might want to include a workbook. These can be hard copy or downloadable PDF files.

Either way they are a proven way to improve engagement with your presentation content, and there is research to show that people who actually use and write in your workbooks, are more likely to engage directly with you after the event. It's a fact.

Whilst you may want to include a workbook as part of your seminar, webinar or even school presentation, you can also turn your workbook or handout into a standalone product which you sell separately.

Two years ago, I gave a presentation to a school, and included a ten page 'pamphlet' as an accompanying handout. I've subsequently been asked for copies of it by other schools, so I have added additional content and now sell it as a print-on-demand book. It will also be available on the Kindle shortly and as a downloadable eGuide on my website.

Because it is a print-on-demand book, I can also customise the cover to each school.

So from starting out as a handout, it has been repurposed into three products that I can sell. There will be a fourth soon when I turn it into a webinar which will be sold to schools around the world. Not to mention the audio version…

PHILIP CALVERT

Financial Services speaker and consultant Bill Bachrach has for many years provided a very simple but highly effective 'Roadmap' handout to clients as part of his training and consultancy, but he also sells it separately as a high value product. Any financial adviser could create something similar which can either be given to clients as a piece of added value, but you could just as easily create something and sell it to clients and prospects in a variety of ways. I'll expand on this later.

You don't need to have any fancy graphic skills either. Just take expertise and values that you have as a financial planner, map it out roughly on a piece of paper and go to Fiverr.com or similar and have someone do the work for you.

Want an example of one I created? The image below is a simple LinkedIn Connection Roadmap showing how people move around and connect on LinkedIn. Although it's really simple, it is a useful giveaway – but also can be included as part of a larger speaking or consulting package.

If you would like the full-size version, just send me an email with the heading 'Roadmap' and I'll send it to you. philip@philipcalvert.com

56 NEW INCOME STREAMS FOR FINANCIAL ADVISERS

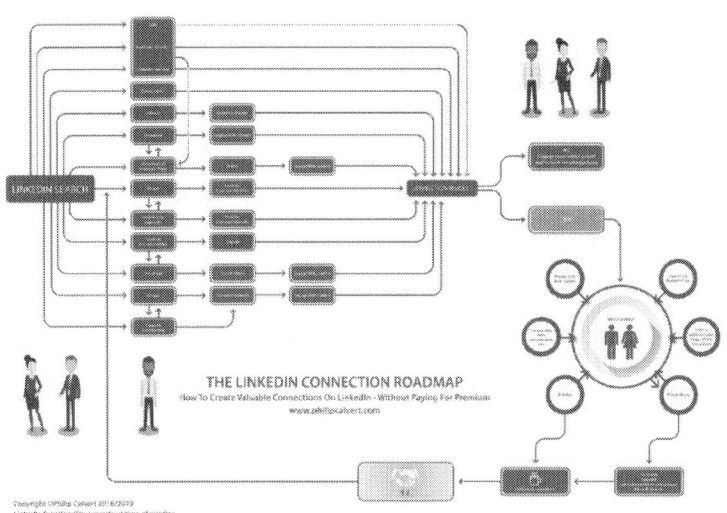

Tips Booklets

If you have created any sort of workbook or handout, it's really easy to repurpose it as a Tips Booklet.

Tips Booklets are really old school, and you probably remember picking these up at the back of the room at conferences and events many years ago.

They were usually a bit smaller than a 9" x 4" envelope, so they could easily be slipped into a jacket pocket. They often looked to be made of average quality card with the pages held together with a staple or simple cotton thread (saddle stitch binding).

Tips Booklets were first popular long before digital printing, but even then, they were pretty cheap to produce at your local printers.

Speakers and seminar leaders would shift these in their hundreds – often as gifts. But the smart speakers realised that they contained value – even if it only had a few pages, so they sold them for anything from under a tenner to three or four times that amount.

What did they contain? Tips – with a call to action at the end.

- Twenty ways to train your dog to…

- Fifteen ways to save money on your household bills…

- Ten proven ways to sell your business at a high price…

- Twenty-five ways to increase the sale value of your home…

- Nineteen ways to find new clients…

You get the idea.

As a financial adviser, you are only limited by your own imagination as to what you could create for your own Tips Booklet. The key is that you keep it simple, with higher value more in-depth content being saved for something else.

Again, you can give your booklet away as a gift, but there will plenty of opportunities when you should/could sell it.

One way I have seen financial advisers selling their Tips Booklet is when they are asked to present to employees in local companies and offer bulk copies which have been customised with the company's logo.

On one occasion the adviser was paid by the client company to present to employees and gave the booklets away as part of the event. On another I've known the adviser to speak for free but offer customised booklets to all employees for a modest fee.

It's your booklet – you decide how you want to monetise it.

How long will it take you to write your Tips Booklet?

Not much more than an hour, maybe two maximum.

Remember that this is a very specific design of Tips Booklet – simple, pocket sized and inexpensive to produce. It doesn't even need any fancy graphics on the front – keep it plain with just your company name and the title of the contents. If you wish, you could include your company logo and website and maybe a client's logo too if you've had it customised.

With today's printing technology, you could of course go very fancy with your design, and that's fine – but better suited to something else like a 'Mini Book' that you might want to produce. We'll talk about Mini Books later.

eBooks

EBooks are now the Daddy of the online information sales market. They are relatively easy to produce and can bring in significant levels of revenue. They are your first step into the world of self-publishing, which we explore further later.

They are also the easiest product to create and produce the highest profit.

In addition to bringing in income, like a 'real' book, eBooks can also position you as the expert on a topic, or at least someone who has expertise or skills in a given area.

The first thing to know is that eBooks do not have to be 'full length' with hundreds of pages, but they do need to contain quality information. Many people use them as lead magnets on their website to encourage visitors to leave their email address, whilst others sell them as products in their own right.

Yes, you can write an eBook in very little time at all, and there are plenty of people selling information online as to how you can 'knock one out' in a few hours. Each to their own, but I can't imagine that any professional financial adviser would want to put something out that is of substandard quality.

What is an eBook?

At the end of the day it's anything you want it to be. Yes, it can be a full-length novel that you make available in a digital format, but it can also be a PDF information product with just a handful of pages.

Either way, you must first think where it will sit on your Value Ladder. Is it something cheap and simple that you are giving away as a lead magnet, or is it something of higher value that people will be prepared to pay for?

You also need to think about what you are trying to achieve with it. For example, is it something that provides information, but which encourages the reader to take the next step and then ask for your help – or is it a solution to a specific problem in its own right? In short, it could be both but ultimately, it's up to you.

Take the eBook that you are reading right now (assuming you are reading the Kindle or PDF version)…

There is enough information for any reader to implement and benefit from its suggestions, but some people will invariably ask me for help.

Creating your eBook

Broadly speaking you have two main options when creating an eBook:

You create your text on a Word document (or equivalent), convert it into a PDF file and sell or promote through your website or funnel.

Or your text is made available on the Kindle device.

Yes, there are other e-readers (like Kobo), but for ease and simplicity it's best to start with PDF and/or Kindle.

One thing worth bearing in mind about eBooks is that you don't have to have an ISBN (International Standard Book Number), even when publishing on the Kindle, though many people do. The point about eBooks is that you can literally write your text and you've got your product, regardless of where you are promoting it.

(However, if you are also creating a hard copy of your eBook, it will need a different ISBN number if it was published with one as an eBook. I.e. each format of your book needs its own ISBN number if you are going down that route.)

So in theory, you can write your text and be selling it in a matter of hours – keeping in mind what I said about quality earlier.

You should also get some cover artwork for your eBook. You don't need to employ the services of a professional graphic designer, but even if you do, there are sites like Fiverr.com where you can get the work done relatively inexpensively. That said if you are creating a very high-quality eBook, then you may want to invest in the services of a book cover professional.

There are other tools like Canva where you can use readymade book cover templates and modify them for your needs.

Some people like to have 3D versions of their cover for promotion on their website, and these make what is actually a PDF file 'look' like a real book. Simply search for eCover Generators or eCover Creators and you'll find a range of online DIY services to help you.

You will also find an increasing number of services which will convert your text or even a blog into an eBook in an instant with lots of fancy graphics. And you'll also find some services where people can see the pages turn like in a real book. Again, it's up to you but if you're getting started a PDF of your written text is just fine – there's no need to overcomplicate things.

Traditionally the PDF version of eBooks has dominated the market, but today Amazon's Kindle format is growing rapidly. And being on Amazon means that you can benefit from the massive distribution opportunity that is available.

Shoppers on Amazon can also use the 'Look Inside' feature, so they can see a sample of your eBook before they buy.

If you are including the Kindle as an option for your eBook, your text needs to be formatted for the device. Again, you can find someone on Fiverr to do it for you, or once again Amazon can help with its tool Kindle Create at:

http://bit.ly/KindleCreateLink

There's also an explanatory video at
https://youtu.be/Fvq1M1HsCrE

Amazon book covers are not currently shown in 3D, so you'll also need to get a flat version of your artwork for uploading with your text.

What should you write about in your eBook?

Again – anything!

But as mentioned earlier, do think about where this product sits on your Value Ladder and also who you are targeting. But as a rule of thumb, the best eBooks address a very real problem that you know your target clients have.

eBooks that show 'how to' solve a problem work well, as do those which solve an urgent issue.

Tom, a speaker friend of mine once wrote an eBook on how to write a wedding speech. It sold well but did even better when he started writing ready-made wedding toasts (which were usually purchased on Friday afternoons).

He's also written one called *Instant Eulogy Speeches*, and both eBooks have brought in hundreds of thousands of dollars for him over the years.

Try to focus your content on solutions to help people:

- Save time
- Save or make more money
- Avoid effort or pain
- How to get a faster or easier result
- How to increase personal status

Take the eBook you are reading right now…

Its goal is to help financial advisers find easy ways to make more money using their expertise, skills and experience. And in so doing suggests ideas to gradually move away from the regulated environment.

Another good format for eBooks is to interview someone. The interview format is particularly popular and easy to do. Find an expert or someone of interest who has appeal to your target audience, interview them, transcribe and publish. It is literally that easy.

If you can interview one person a month for a year, you could create twelve eBooks! Or, create one large one.

Other ideas for eBooks include:

Create a compendium of your blogs

The 'How to do XYZ' format

How to Do X In…

How to Get or Do X Without Doing Y

How to Easily…

How to X in A Week

'Getting started' with XYZ

'Step by Step' Guides To…

The Two Minutes a Day Guide To…

ABC Demystified…

'Top Twenty' ways to…

Ten Ways to Be More…

Fifteen Things You Need to Know About X To…

'Thirty days' to…

Instant X

The Ten Must Have Tools To…

The Twenty Best Websites To…

'Top ten' mistakes made by…

What I Wish I Knew Before I…

My Journey To…

The Ultimate Guide To…

Twelve Must-Read Books On (Topic)

The Financial Adviser's Guide To…

The Adviser's Blueprint To…

A Proven Plan To…

An Advanced Guide To…

How to Get the Most Out of Your…

Time Sensitive Topics

Etc.

According to Amazon, the most popular eBooks cover the following topics:

- Business & Money
- Self-Help
- Cookbooks, Food & Wine
- Politics & Social Sciences
- Health, Fitness & Dieting
- Parenting & Relationships
- Crafts, Hobbies & Home
- Education & Teaching

Create a Compelling Title

It should go without saying that the title of your eBook is critical and creating a good one is an art in itself. Always think about who you are targeting it at and make the title as relevant as possible to their needs and problems.

Again, technology can help us here, and there is an amazing software called Funnel Scripts which creates titles and marketing copy automatically.

It's based on thousands of the world's most effective titles and is astonishing in what it can do. It's not cheap, but as well as being ideal for coming up with great titles, it is also extremely useful for creating other types of copy that you use in your business such as marketing materials, emails, advertisements, website copy, PowerPoint slides etc.

Take a look at http://bit.ly/FSTitleScripts

Out of all the ideas in this book, you may well find that creating and selling your own eBook is ultimately the easiest and most profitable. The day you sell your first eBook is very exciting and you'll wish you had done it years ago – so why not get started today…

Audio Books

The next logical step after creating your eBook, is to make the audio version of it and sell that too.

Sometimes eBook writers will sell the eBook and the audio version as a package – or they might give away the eBook free but then offer the audio version as a chargeable upsell.

There are also specific benefits to producing an Audio Book over and above an eBook or normal physical book, not least of which are:

- It can be listened to on the go – at the gym, in the car etc.

- Increased profit – some people prefer to listen to a book than read it

- Can be included with other products as part of a broader, more profitable package

- Reach a different audience – including people who are blind or dyslexic

- Zero printing costs

- You'll never run out of stock

- Audio books add to your digital footprint and give people another way to find you and your expertise

In an ideal world, you will want to record your audio in a studio environment, but these days a good quality microphone is well within the reach of most people. Any of the Blue Yeti or Snowball microphones will do the job, which just plug into your laptop or PC.

Just make sure that the room where you do your recording has no distracting noises and without any echo at all. Cushions and curtains in the room are your friend here or you can create a simple recording area with some inexpensive soundproofing panels from Amazon.

The sound does need to be clear and without background distractions, because many people will listen to it on headphones or in their car – but again, as long as it reaches at least that bar, you don't need to hire Abbey Road Studios.

You might also want some simple editing software which may already be installed on your computer, or failing that something like Audacity is available free at www.audacityteam.org/download/.

There are plenty of beginner and advanced Audacity tutorials on YouTube, or once again put any editing that's needed out to someone on Fiverr. But to be honest, it's pretty easy to learn in a very short period of time. You can always ask your kids to help...

Once you've got your MP3 audio file of your eBook you are good to go. If you want to get fancy you may want to have the file hosted somewhere like you would do for a Podcast, but for most audio books it's easy enough to put the file in DropBox or Google Drive and then give your customers a link to it. This can be automated, or you can just email them a link.

Another option is to pre-load an MP3 player and mail it out to purchasers.

Hopefully you are getting the message by now that this stuff is really quite easy to do. Creating your own products might sound complicated, but it really need not be. Most people find the hardest bit is just deciding to create something and then get started.

Physical Books - Published

Writing a book is often seen as the Holy Grail of information products. Trust me when I tell you that when you first see and hold your own book in your hands is an amazing moment.

But while it's sitting in your hands and you're now calling yourself a published author, your book is worthless to you. You've got to get it out there and push it like crazy for it to be of any benefit to you.

Let's start this section with some benefits of financial advisers writing a book:

- Enhances your visibility – positions you as an expert in your field

- Increases your status

- Adds a physical product to your list of services

- Enhances your credibility within your industry or profession

- Has the potential to increase your financial advice fees

- Fantastic PR

- Attracts speaking and consulting business

- Attracts pre-qualified client prospects

- Raises your profile locally

- Personal branding

- Increases self-confidence

- Improves your planning skills

- Opens unexpected doors

- Attracts new networking opportunities

- Improves your writing skills in all aspects of your life and business

- Expands your content marketing opportunities through re-purposing of individual sections within the book

- Creates a new income stream

There are multiple techniques for getting your book a lot of visibility and onto the Amazon best-seller lists, but that's not within the scope of this guide. My job is to convince you that writing a book is a powerful and valuable thing for a financial adviser to do – not least of which because it differentiates you from other advisers, and in a big way.

Very few authors of business or personal development related books make a LOT of money from them, but they do create an income stream in their own right and are great door openers and sweeteners for other work that you do. Just like the Tips Booklets I talked about earlier, there are various things you can do with your book.

Make money from sales on bookstores and online, give them away as gifts, offer them as part of a consultancy or speaking package – and who knows, if it sells well you could always sell the rights to a production company. But let's not run until we can walk!

For many authors of 'how to' type products, your book becomes your business card and leads to other things such as consultancy, radio and TV appearances and speaking work.

Very often, your book is also a lead magnet for your other higher proceed offerings on your Value Ladder.

Do Financial Advisers write Books?

In the USA, many have done so, but here in the UK very few have taken this step. But to name a few, Martin Bamford has three published personal finance books to his name - *The Money Tree*, *How to Retire Ten Years Early* and *Brilliant Investing* – plus *Ready, Steady, Retire!* which was co-authored with another financial planner Justin King of MFP Wealth Management in Christchurch, Dorset.

Jason Butler, formerly of Bloomsbury has three published books to his name, plus one co-authored with others.

Others from the profession who you will know who are published authors include Abraham Okusanya, George Kinder, Chris Budd, Nick Murray, Tony Granger, Pete Matthew, Rebecca Robertson, Warren Shute, Dennis Hall, Brian Butcher and Anita Gatehouse to name a few. But there aren't many more...

How 'difficult' is it to write a Book?

There are some international best sellers that were written in a matter of hours, whilst others can take (literally) years. One thing that holds back a lot of people is that they feel it has to be perfect before it sees the light of day, and as a result it never does.

But with technology comes new ways to make the process easier. Clearly you need to be sure that there is a market for your book, but 'putting pen to paper' need not be hard work.

Many authors will use voice recognition software which automatically transcribes your words, and this approach can massively speed up the creation process.

Or, you could hire a ghost writer who interviews you and then does the writing for you.

At the end of the day, writing a book is about getting your ideas and content written down. Getting it out to the masses is another matter, but it's my job to put the idea about writing one in the first place into your head.

There are a multitude of websites, videos, blogs and courses that will teach you the structure of writing a book, and I can even introduce you to people who will coach you, hold your hand and hold you accountable. In other words, they'll make sure that you get it done.

It can indeed seem a little daunting when you first make the decision to write a book, but once you have made a start, your brain will have focus and help you to get it finished. With coaching, you'll get it finished sooner and the quality will be higher.

In addition to hiring a ghost writer, you can also use technology in other ways. Remember those twelve interviews I mentioned earlier? The interview format is becoming increasingly popular, and with transcription software it is easier than ever before to bring your book to market.

Sitting on my bookshelf is a book called *30 Days*. It is a large, heavy hardback book containing 543 pages of transcriptions of video interviews with thirty leading internet marketers, each describing how they would build an internet marketing business from scratch in just thirty days. It is worth its weight in gold.

Transcribing interviews is a powerful but ridiculously simple way to create a book of high value which you can sell in a variety of ways and add significant value to your proposition – not to mention your bank balance.

Who could you interview for such a book?

- Yourself(!)
- Local businesspeople
- Other business leaders
- Economists
- Futurists
- Academics
- Business and professional speakers
- Topic experts
- Other authors
- Professional connections

- Journalists
- High achievers, sports people etc.
- Clients
- Connections on LinkedIn (people LOVE to be asked to be interviewed)

The list is endless.

How do I get it published?

For some strange reason, this question is one of the things that actually stops people from putting pen to paper in the first place. Yes, we've all heard stories of authors being rejected by publishers hundreds of times, and sure, that must be pretty soul-destroying.

But it doesn't need to be that way in this day and age.

What is important though is that you have a basic understanding of the publishing market and what publishers are looking for. At its most basic, they are looking to make a profit. Period.

When you present your book to a publisher, they are going to need to see a few things:

- Is there a market for your book?

- How is your book different from other books on this topic?

- Why and how are you qualified to write this book?

- What else have you written – like a blog (not essential but a big help)

- Do you already have a following who will buy it?

- Where are the opportunities for bulk purchases (like clubs and associations)?

- How could you help with the marketing and promotion?

- Will the book sell in international markets?

- Are you willing to speak on the topic at events and conferences?

- Are you willing to be interviewed by journalists?

In short, you need to convince them that your book is worth their time, energy, enthusiasm, investment and commitment.

Generally speaking, it is the job of the publisher to publish and distribute the book, and depending on a variety of factors, they will also do some, but not a lot of marketing.

If you are perhaps Lee Child or Robert Cialdini, they'll do a lot more. So they will look much more favourably on your proposal if you have your own promotional plan at the ready.

Don't just start Writing

When I first sat down to write a book, my instinct was to plan it and then just start writing. Turns out that's not a very good idea if you want to go down the publisher route.

One of the first things I discovered was that it is almost always better to write a book proposal or synopsis first, before you write the book itself.

I can think of few things more depressing than having sweated blood over the manuscript, to be told by fifty publishers that they are not interested – and each for a different reason. And just as bad, is being told that the subject matter is a "great idea Phil", but that you should re-write most of it – again for a whole host of different reasons.

Far better, is to put a proposal to a publisher first, providing detailed information about what you plan to write – not what you have already written.

Trust me, whilst you still have to put real effort into your proposal, it will take nothing like as much effort as the book itself and will save you heartache later.

Having made your proposal to the publisher, they can then tell you if they like it, and if so, how best you should approach it.

A word of advice here, which I have already hinted at earlier. Take the comments of the publisher seriously and with good grace. Remember, they know best about what will or will not sell and be prepared to compromise.

The chances are, they will give you some additional ideas to include which:

a) you won't have thought of yourself, and b) will make the book more saleable either at home or abroad.

If you want to write a book that is exactly how you want it – without editorial interference, then publish it yourself. However, if you write your proposal well and can show why your book will sell, more often than not you will have a reasonably free hand.

Don't expect to have too much input into things like the cover and its design, but if you strike up a good relationship with the publisher right from the start and can show them that you are 'keen', then you will enjoy being part of the process.

In fact, even though the publisher will have their own contacts that look after the design process, quite often they will work with specific people that you recommend. For example, my brother David is a professional photographer and took the photos for the cover of my first book. Another photographer I know provided the cover images for my second book.

As far as the title of your book is concerned, different publishers take different approaches. Don't be surprised (or offended) if the publisher chooses a title of his or her own for your book.

And, if you are fortunate enough to be commissioned to write a specific book, it is likely that you will be given the title in advance.

In short, the book proposal is your sales document, your pitch. It's your chance to convince the publisher that you have got something special.

Should you go through a Publisher or Literary Agent?

Firstly, you need to decide to whom you will be sending your book proposal. Will you go direct to the publisher, or will you go through a literary agent?

Using the services of a literary agent is well worth considering. Why? Because they know the world of publishing inside out. They know exactly which publishers are most likely to be interested in your topic. But please note, literary agents are not a shortcut to getting published. They apply the same exacting standards as publishers – sometimes more so.

The services of a literary agent can be extremely valuable, particularly if your area of expertise is very niche – like financial services. Bear in mind that they too will want to see a detailed proposal before even looking at you.

Naturally, they charge for their services, but they could make the difference between being published or not. Before approaching such an agent, you should check to see if they specialise in a particular area.

For example, there is little point in sending a proposal for a book on Pension Planning to an agent that specialises in (say) Horror. Well, maybe...

Also bear in mind that literary agents receive many hundreds of enquiries each month, so do not follow up your enquiry for several weeks. Whilst I am advocating the submission of a book proposal to literary agents, do check in advance, as some prefer a letter or email in the first instance.

Some literary agents may also charge you a 'reading fee'. I liken this to speaker bureaus that make a charge to professional speakers for looking at their promotional materials and putting them on their list/register. It is my personal opinion that you should not feel the need to pay such a fee, as there are a great many agents who do not charge.

At the end of the day, it is up to you and the budget you have available, but a well-written book proposal in which either a publisher or an agent can see clear benefits of proceeding with the project, should stand on its own merits and not after the payment of a fee.

Whether you use a literary agent or go direct to the publisher, just make sure that your letter or proposal is smart and professional and without typos! The coming pages will reveal exactly what should go into your proposal.

Writing your Proposal and Synopsis

Let's now look at the key components of your book proposal/synopsis.

You can include additional information if you wish, but the following elements are a must:

1. The Overview (or Introduction)

2. Summary of the Chapters and the Table of Contents

3. Market Summary and Analysis

4. Your Experience and Credibility

5. How you will be Promoting the Book

6. Two Sample Chapters

Let's look at each in turn.

1. The Overview (or Introduction)

As the opening section of the proposal, there are certain key elements that need to be included. In short, they are:

a) Who the book is for

b) Why they are going to buy it, and

c) Why you are the person to write it.

From these three points alone, the publisher (or agent) should be able to see instantly why they should support the project. If they can't see the benefits to the reader and to themselves, they will stop there. So, if you don't get this bit right, you might as well not bother.

What else should be included in the Overview?

At the heart of the Overview is your research and your evidence of research – i.e. The main statistics that prove why your book is needed or the basis for your presumption that the book will sell. You should summarise the concept behind your book and the main point that you will be making within it.

You should be able to show that you have read other books (i.e. competitors' books) and that you know your subject inside out. At this stage of the proposal you do not need to go into the detail of how your book will be different, but it should be clear as to how you will be adding to the 'genre' or niche.

In some respects, your overview is likely to be quite similar to the actual Introduction in the book itself. In other words, you are setting the tone for the remainder of the proposal and the book.

Be prepared for the publisher to ask you for proof that the market you say is out there, is actually there. For example, are you making assumptions that there is a market for your book, or have you actually tested it with research? It is better to assume that you will be asked for this, rather than to wait for them to ask or even hope they won't.

Not only will a publisher expect to see evidence that there is a market for your book, they may even ask for proof that they will buy it. Have you got advance orders or statements of interest in writing?

Finally, if it isn't already evident from the research you are presenting, you should include brief information to show why you are the person to be writing the book.

What proof have you got that you are the expert you say you are? Keep that one in mind as you write your Overview. And if there are other experts in the field, what sets you apart from them, or how are you different?

Also keep in mind that this information will be used as part of the promotional activities such as Press Releases.

In summary, your Overview should reveal benefits. Benefits for the reader and benefits for the publisher.

For the reader, you must be able to show how the book will help them, their bank balance, their love life, their promotion prospects and so on.

Equally, the publisher must be able to see how easy it will be for them to sell the book and to make a profit. Sometimes, they will also be looking for a series of books, and if you believe your subject matter will be suitable, make it clear how you can help them in future.

2. Summary of the Chapters and Table of Contents

At this point, you will have had to think about the actual content of the book, down to the level of detail of what will be in each chapter. The number of chapters will vary, but as a rule of thumb for the purposes of the proposal, twelve is as good a number as any. Twelve will satisfy the publisher that you have enough material, whilst not overwhelming him or her with the depth of your knowledge.

Whilst this is a 'formal' synopsis/proposal, you will invariably find that when you come to actually write the book, you are likely to have either more or less material and chapters than you originally planned. Don't worry, the publisher is unlikely to hold you to exactly what you put in your synopsis, as long as you deliver the key themes and benefits that you promised.

In any event, the publisher will read your final manuscript, as will their editor and around three proof-readers, so plenty of people will be checking that your book 'delivers'.

In my own experience, I have tended to overdo the number of chapters in the synopsis/proposal and end up amalgamating some of them in the final text.

One of the most important things to remember however, is that the chapter contents/titles appear to have a logical order. Even someone who is not familiar with your subject or area of expertise, should be able to see a logical sequence of titles. If the publisher is confused by your synopsis of the chapters, it will make them less inclined to take on your book – or at least until you can make it clearer.

What comes first – Chapter titles or the Content?

Personally, I have the book 'in my head' so it's quite easy to come up with working titles for each chapter and which are clear enough for the publisher in the synopsis. These working titles then act as headings and provide some structure for me to write around. I can then fine-tune the chapter titles later.

How much detail is required?

Aim for about three paragraphs to describe each chapter. In my view, it doesn't matter how technical your topic is – you should still be able to summarise each chapter in three paragraphs. If you can't get across the main point of each chapter in three paragraphs, plus maybe a half dozen summary bullet points, it's possible that the chapter itself may not have been thought through clearly enough.

Occasionally, if you feel it is appropriate, and it helps to make a very important point that is central to the book, by all means include some 'real' examples, stories or anecdotes – perhaps some that you will actually be using in the book.

In short, this section of your synopsis, is giving the publisher a 'feel' for your book, without them actually having to read the book in full. If you can imagine how many enquiries publishers receive on a weekly basis, you will see that it is completely impractical for them to read every book that is sent to them.

Do yourself, and them a favour and write a clear, well thought through synopsis, which is just that – a synopsis. The publisher's experience will tell them straight away whether your project is worth them running with.

Finally, don't pitch the technical level of your chapter overview too high, unless you are writing a very technical manual – in which case you will be talking to a specialist publisher.

3. Market Summary and Analysis

This is another important part of the proposal, as it starts to show that you have done your homework, and that you are aware of how your proposed book will sit within the marketplace.

In other words, not only will you show the publisher that you know what the competition is, but also that you are thinking about how your book will be or needs to be different from everything else.

And believe me, it does need to be different – or at least adds to the body of work that is already available on your subject.

Being different will make your book stand out from the crowd, and so make it potentially easier for the publisher to sell. Another point to remember is that people who have already bought books on your subject matter, will be likely to buy yet another (i.e. yours), if they can see that it takes a different slant from the books they already have.

Buying business books, self-help books or personal development books can be a bit of a habit for some people, so dare I suggest that you aim to feed their craving!

So the essence of this section of the synopsis, is to show how your book will be different, better, more in depth, more effective and so on.

Do not be afraid to list out competitive books in your sector. The publisher needs to know what other books on your subject are out there, so they can see how well they sell, how they are promoted and how yours will be different. This will also show the publisher that you know your market.

You don't know your market? If not, why not? How can you profess to be an expert on your subject if you haven't read all the other books that are available?

Once you have listed out all the other main books on your subject, write an outline of the top half dozen or so. That means you need to have read them! Or, at least have familiarised yourself with their contents, themes and ideas.

And yes, Amazon is a good place to do this, as there are very often some good descriptions. Bear in mind though, that the authors themselves write many of the descriptions of books on Amazon – so ideally you should read the books yourself.

In short, be thorough in your research of the market. Your outline of each of the other books should be around three paragraphs in length.

Paragraph #1

Outline the positive aspects of each competitor's book, describing the themes and key points it is making. You may also include any information you have available on its sales figures and/or interesting information about the author.

For example:

Has he or she appeared on television talking about their book?

Is there public demand for information on their subject?

Is your subject matter currently trendy (like a new diet etc.)?

In other words, show the publisher that your book has the potential to achieve similar positive publicity.

Don't be afraid to praise the book if it's good. By saying how a book is good, may help to reaffirm why another, albeit slightly different book (i.e. yours), will feed the demand for further material on the subject.

Paragraph #2

Highlight why the book concerned does not, in your view go far enough or does not address certain issues or fulfil its promises.

Do not be rude about someone else's book. It may be a competitor, but this is not a competition. Be professional at all times in your critique – you are not writing a review in the Sunday Times Literary Supplement.

Paragraph #3

Suggest how your book will be different or better, and how it will more closely meet the needs of your target audience.

Here, you can now start to lay it on thickly as to the benefits of your book over the others.

Remember – benefits, benefits, benefits – for the reader and the publisher. Keep this in mind all the time as you write your synopsis/proposal.

As part of the analysis section, you can also suggest some ideas on how you envisage the layout of your book – but only in so much that it will make certain points more clearly if they are presented (say) diagrammatically.

Do not expect to have too much input into the physical design of the book. Yes, make some suggestions by all means, but trust the publisher's own opinions.

As mentioned earlier, it's also worth keeping in mind that they might not even go with your choice of title for the book. Again, don't be distressed by this and just go with the flow. Very often, you will be given the title for the book if and when you reach contract stage after they have seen your synopsis.

Remember – you may be the expert on the content of the book, but the publisher is the expert on what it looks like, what it says on the cover and how it will fit into the marketplace.

Conclude your competitor analysis with a brief summary. It should sing out a specific benefit for the reader, from which the publisher should be able to see how your book will be different from the competition and why it will sell.

4. Your Experience and Credibility

As we said at the beginning, credibility is everything. Whilst your idea for the book may sound great, new and exciting, the publisher will need to know that you are indeed an expert on your subject. The last thing they want on their hands is a string of reviews from other experts saying that the contents of your book are unfounded and unproven nonsense.

Even worse, is if your book gives specific advice, which is incorrect and results in (say) financial loss for its readers. Naturally, you will want to consider running your book past a compliance expert in certain circumstances.

So, you will need to prove that you are who you say you are, and that you are in fact an expert on your subject – if not *the* expert.

In this section of the synopsis, don't go over-the-top in your description of yourself. Stick to the facts but show how your expertise has been applied in the past. Perhaps you have appeared on radio or TV, or you are a speaker or lecturer on your subject.

Can you show published articles that you have written, or articles about you that have been written in the Press? The more 'national' the Press, the better but if you can show articles that feature your expertise in specialist magazines and papers like Money Marketing, FT Adviser, Citywire etc., that will be fine.

Testimonials are also important, and if they are from someone famous, that will help. (If you include any testimonials in your synopsis/proposal, make sure you have permission to use them.)

The publisher may even ask you to approach your famous fan for a comment, which could go on the front cover of the book.

Naturally, your qualifications will need to be highlighted and your experience in your industry. In short, this is your chance to say why you are the person to be writing this book.

5. How you will promote the book

This should be the easiest section of the synopsis/proposal, because presumably you want it to sell by the skip load.

Do not assume that just because you have a book deal, that it will sell. The world is a big place and there are a lot of books out there. Why should yours sell simply because it has a new approach to a particular subject?

It will need promoting, and don't expect the publisher to do all the work. Many authors are quite surprised when they don't see their work in any bookshops and start to question what the publishers are up to. Yes, they do some promotion, and depending on who you are (amongst other things), they will only have a certain amount of budget to get the book out there.

So, they will be expecting you to put in some effort as well, and if nothing else, this section of the synopsis will start you thinking about a promotional plan.

It's not for me to say what should be in your promotional plan – it's your book and you should know who is likely to buy it. So at the very least, aim for your book to be the dominating publication in your market. It's well worth taking this attitude if you are going down the publisher route.

This means careful targeting. Consider all the different ways that you could promote your book to your target market, and then, depending on your budget, decide how best you will reach people.

PR may be an option, radio advertising another. Whatever you do, write a plan and share it with the publisher. Help them and they will be more inclined to help you.

A good tip is to get a Twitter account going well in advance which is based around the topic or theme of your book. That way a publisher will be able to see that you are serious, and that people are already engaging with your tweets.

You could also set up a dedicated Facebook or LinkedIn group, and start to build community around your topic. Then, when your book is launched, you can promote it within your ready-made community of followers.

On the subject of building community around you and your topic, you may also wish to consider creating a chargeable group using a platform like Mighty Networks. Alternatively, you could make your group free to join, but then charge for courses based around your topic.

Essentially, we want to show a publisher that there is already interest or demand for your expertise, and clearly social media and online groups are a simple but powerful way to do this.

Also, get out on the speaking circuit. The book will help you to get gigs, and the gigs will help you to sell books. You will sell them either at the back of the room after your talks, or online.

Even if you have just given the best talk ever on your subject, many people will not purchase the book there and then – even if it does mean missing out on getting an autographed copy! They will prefer to buy it from an online bookshop in their own time (and perhaps cheaper).

By the way, I have also noticed that every time I give a talk, workshop or keynote on the topics within my books, my rankings on Amazon always improve the next day.

Another way to show a publisher that you mean business is to start a podcast based around your topic. There are a variety of formats for podcasts, any of which could work for you:

1. Solo shows with just you speaking

2. Interview format where you interview a guest during your show

3. Conversations – less of an interview and more of a chat

4. Either of 2) and 3) above but with several people – like a panel

5. FAQs – audience's questions

6. Best practices and success stories

7. A mixture of all of the above

An author will often start a podcast *after* their book is published, but it's also well worth starting one *before*, which can later be enhanced by the appearance of your book.

It's worth reiterating the benefits of having your own podcast, and if you put yourself in the shoes of a publisher, you can see why it's important in support of your book proposal:

- It gives you instant credibility and influence

- It builds your 'fan base' or community

- Podcasts reach new audiences you haven't seen before

- Grows an audience of prospects for your book

- It establishes expertise and trust with your audience

- It attracts enquiries for your products and services

- Builds up a valuable library of content

- Your content is available on demand, night or day

- Your content can be consumed on the go (cars, trains, at the gym etc.)

- Attracts speaking engagements

- Attracts press interviews

- Well-connected people will often take your call when they know you are a podcast host

- You can take advertising and sponsorships and thus build strategic alliances with those who could promote your book

- Podcasts often open unexpected doors for your services

- Listeners often share specific episodes to their friends and social media contacts

And don't forget that podcast hosts often get asked to appear on other people's podcasts – further broadening your reach.

Having a podcast is not essential as part of your pitch to a publisher, but you can clearly see that there are very specific benefits which will be attractive to them. Equally, if you had your own YouTube channel which posts regular content around your expertise in a topic, you can see how that would also be of benefit in supporting your book proposal.

Whilst I said this is potentially the easiest part of your synopsis, it is also extremely important. Neither you nor the publisher will be particularly pleased if it doesn't sell.

Make sure you have a plan in place (written) and with measurable goals. Again, this will show the publisher that you are serious, and that you will be helping them to get a return on their investment.

6. Two Sample Chapters

Sample chapters are important for a variety of different reasons, not least of which is for the publisher to get a feel for your writing style and a sense of what the book is really all about.

And, although your final manuscript will be checked and double checked before it goes anywhere near the printers, the publisher will also be looking to see how you present your material. Is it full of errors? Does it 'sit' well on the page? Is it readable? Can you make a relatively complex subject like financial planning easy to understand?

A synopsis is all well and good, but a chapter or two will help to bring it to life for the publisher. As I have said earlier, they do not want to read the whole book before they say "yes please" (or "no thanks" for that matter). The synopsis is a concise 'short cut' for the publisher, and through their extensive experience, this document will be sufficient for them to decide if this is worth their time and attention – i.e. whether or not it will sell!

In my synopsis for *Successful Seminar Selling* I decided to include the Introduction as one of my specimen chapters, and the first chapter as the other. Different publishers have different requirements and you do not necessarily have to include the first two. You can choose any chapters, but the Introduction is a very good scene setter.

Your other chapter should ideally be your favourite one. Or, if you haven't written anything yet, write the chapter that you think best reveals your passion for the subject, or the most amount of expertise. To be simplistic – send in the best bits.

But again, always keep in mind that the publisher will be looking for the benefits to them. Will they see practical and useful stuff which will be invaluable to readers?

Treat your specimen chapters very seriously. Present them properly with double (or 1.5) spaced lines. And for the avoidance of doubt, that means typed and on decent paper! Yes, many will accept PDFs by email, but publishing can be relatively old-fashioned so play the game.

Make it easy to read and use a Serif font – and don't make it too small.

Never send in a handwritten synopsis. Make sure there are no spelling mistakes or grammatical errors and have a proof-reader go through it in fine detail. I don't think I need to explain why, do I?

As I said earlier, these are unlikely to be final versions of the chapters, but they will be sufficient for the publisher to get to know what you and your proposed book are all about. And if nothing else, you will have at least started writing the book.

Finish with a Summary

So, we have written the bulk of the synopsis with six key elements. Round it off with a concluding paragraph. Not too long - more a brief 'signing off' statement which sums up everything you have said. And remember; try to put yourself in the shoes of the publisher. Can they see benefits, benefits, benefits?

And there it is – you've written your proposal. A key document on the way to getting your book published.

Finally, write a short and to-the-point covering letter (or email). Enclose the covering letter with your synopsis in a large envelope. Don't fold it.

Find out exactly to whom it should be sent and address it to them in person. Make absolutely sure that you spell their name right...

If you follow the synopsis formula, you will be making the process of getting a publishing deal very much easier for yourself.

And what's the evidence for this?

You'll remember that I had previously sat down to start writing my first book, and with very little planning. But when I was about three chapters in, I noticed an event being promoted in London called *How to Get Published by the Very First Publisher you Approach.*

It was being hosted by the top US literary agent Wendy Keller, who only takes on nonfiction work by established experts, thought leaders, media personalities, scientists, leading businesspeople and those who are well-positioned in their respective fields. She only takes them on through referral from existing authors on her books.

PHILIP CALVERT

I didn't tick any of those boxes, and it was very expensive to attend – but the opportunity to spend a day with Wendy was too good to miss. Maybe I'd pick up a couple of tips…

Let's put it this way; I returned from Wendy's workshop and threw my entire manuscript straight into the bin. I then proceeded to follow every single word of her training, and to cut a long story short, ended up having my first book accepted by the very first publisher that I approached – and on the first day that they read my proposal.

They didn't ask for any changes and fell over themselves to help me bring the book to life.

Six months later my publisher approached me to commission the writing of a second book, which also resulted in me promoting it on BBC Breakfast television.

The steps I have highlighted in this section of this book, are the very steps that Wendy taught me on her workshop. I hope they will work for you too.

Don't forget that you can approach a Literary Agent directly. Check out the Writers and Artists Year Book at www.writersandartists.co.uk which is an amazing resource, plus Google to find lists of them - or look in the acknowledgments section of similar books to your own to find relevant names.

LinkedIn is a good place to look too. I just ran a search for Literary Agent and over 24,000 came up in the results – over 2,000 of whom are in the UK.

It may also be worth attending literary festivals and writers' events to find the right contacts. You should also join online forums where you will find people with the right connections.

Whilst not *essential*, a Literary Agent can be a big help – particularly if your book is very niche. Using their contacts and experience, they can help you to find the right publisher and negotiate the contract on your behalf. Some will also help with the content, structure and style of your book, and may even assist with marketing and promotion ideas.

If you strike up a good relationship, you may even find that some agents will act as a sort of mentor for you and help to develop your new writing career. After all, they are looking for a win, win, win situation for all.

If you can, try to check out the agent's credentials before you approach them. What sort of material do they specialise in? Which other authors have they helped in the same niche as you?

But again, you need to get the attention of the agent in much the same way as you would a publisher. When you first approach an agent, write a short letter asking them what their process is for working with you. This information may also be on their website.

The more clues you can pick up as to how they like to work the better, but at the end of the day, they also need to be able to see whether your book is likely to sell – so the synopsis format will work for most of them as well.

So, there we have it! I've taken much longer over this section because writing a book is potentially a big deal in more ways than one. I hope I have given you some ideas to help you fulfil your dream of seeing your own work on the shelves of the high street bookstores. Oh, and Amazon...

It will add to your credibility as an expert on your subject and may even lead to lucrative speaking fees and overseas travel. It has for me.

For IFAs and other financial advisers, getting a book published is one of the most important things you could do to set you apart from the competition.

Just as we said with your eBook, an audio version of your published book is another opportunity for income. You should discuss this with your publisher.

The Money side of having a Published Book

Different publishers have different approaches to what and how you are paid, and there are still many publishers who pay you once a year. Many won't give you an upfront advance either, so don't get too carried away by the glamour of being a published author.

A lot of first-time authors see the whole process through rose-tinted glasses and are more excited about seeing their book in WH Smith, than what they will actually earn from the project or the doors that it can open.

Many are more than a little surprised to see their book on a shelf in Waterstones or other book store at £12.99 only to end up with £1.10 in royalties for each sale. That's just one example as every publisher's deal is different, so it's important to put this in the context of what you are trying to achieve with your book.

Maybe the money is not the key driver for you and that you are purely using your book as a door opener for other projects. Most professional speakers sell their books in shops, online and at the back of the room at conferences. But more often than not, it is the book that got them the speaking gig in the first place. And that in turn can lead to lucrative inhouse consultancy engagements.

So the alternative to going down the publisher route is to self-publish.

Self-Published books

First let's look at the maths of what is possible, using the earlier example of earning £1.10 on a book that sells for £12.99. Bear in mind too that some publishers will only pay that £1.10 once a year in an annual royalty statement.

Now let's imagine that you published the book yourself and therefore own the rights to it...

In theory you can charge whatever you want for the book, and if you sell it off your website or as a PDF version on your site or funnel, you get 100% of the payment – less a tiny cut if you're using something like PayPal as your payment processors.

Which would you prefer; £1.10 paid once a year, or £12.99 paid immediately?

I am not saying that you shouldn't go down the published route. What I'm suggesting is that before embarking on a book, you should think clearly about your objectives for it and therefore which publishing route is most appropriate for you.

But the self-published route is growing rapidly in popularity amongst authors. The number of self-published books topped the 1 million mark for the first time in 2017, according to Bowker's annual report on the number of ISBNs that were issued to self-published authors. The total number of ISBNs issued last year rose 28% over 2016, to 1,009,188.

Clearly technology has made it easier and easier, and with more and more online services appearing such as Lulu, KDP (Kindle Direct Publishing), CreateSpace, Kobo, AuthorHouse and others, it's easier than ever before to get your work out there. I know authors who have written a book and had it published the same day.

Quite apart from ownership of rights and the financial side of things, one of the main benefits of self-publishing is that you can publish pretty well anything of any length, which can be difficult through the traditional publisher route.

That all said, if you want your work to sell, you should still approach it with much the same discipline and respect as I have described for going down the published route. Just because you have a book to your name, doesn't necessarily mean that you'll sell any, so you should still do your market research, still map out a synopsis and still consider in detail how and where you will sell it.

It's worth bearing in mind that a self-published book can also end up eventually being picked up by a publishing house. Very often a publisher will hear about your book – perhaps through social media, radio, podcasts, TV, blogs or articles etc., and if they like what they see it's not uncommon for them to make you an offer you can't refuse.

This is why it's so important to know your marketplace and the degree to which you have a readymade audience for your book. Whenever a publisher takes on an author and their book, they are essentially taking a punt on whether it will sell. So if they can see that your self-published book is already doing well, then it makes it easier for them to take on your work.

Finally, as mentioned earlier - don't forget to create the audio version of your self-published book. Audio books are rapidly increasing in popularity, so don't miss out on this valuable additional money-making opportunity.

You should ideally voice it yourself, but you can also hire a professional voice artist who will either do it for a fee or a share in the profits. It's up to you.

Case Study Books

Regardless of whether you go down the published or self-published route, one idea that you could try is the Case Study Book.

Also known as Example Books, these are remarkably easy, and often quick to put together. And if they focus on an area of specialism or particular skill, you can charge a lot of money for them.

Quite simply you put together case studies of 'real' client examples, with one case study per chapter. Clearly, you're not going to identify the real clients behind the examples, though permission from the clients concerned would certainly add an extra layer of credibility.

From working with IFAs, mortgage professionals and financial advisers over many years - and from the questions asked by financial planners in our online forums, there is hardly an adviser in the world who doesn't have some great client case studies or stories that could be put in writing over the course of a chapter. I bet you can think of half a dozen right now...

You can make each case study as long or as short as you wish, and even if you managed just six one-page case studies, you will still have created something of real value that you can either give away as a PDF lead magnet on your website, or indeed package up into something more fancy.

One option is to include a range of different case studies as a way to highlight the breadth of the advice or planning you do, or a better option is to focus on a particular type of planning that you offer. For example, case studies that focus on:

- A specific age group

- A specific occupation or niche (e.g. planning for doctors)

- A specific group of people (e.g. executives nearing retirement)

- A specific financial planning issue

- How you have used planning tools – such as cashflow modelling

- How (say) Life Planning has helped clients

Whichever approach you take, it's important that your case studies are real, because 'made up' examples rarely have the same impact.

A technique used by some of the best seminar hosts in Financial Services is to use real case studies as part of their presentation. I've seen a lot of financial advisers' seminars over the years, and the real case studies always seem to have much more credibility than the contrived ones.

The very best presentations I have seen at financial advice seminars are when they use a *live* case study – where the client concerned is in the room.

In addition to case studies, what other data, reports or presentations have you already created (or could create quickly) that you could compile into a book? Do you have before/after testimonials, swipe files, advertisements, PR examples, email newsletters, articles or blogs?

Maybe you have a specific business skill that has helped you to grow your financial advice business over the years. Perhaps you have been particularly successful with podcasts or working with professional connections and introducers. Gather examples together and compile them into a book. Be sure to put a hook in the title to attract your audience.

'Diary of a…' Books

Do you remember the days when the nearest thing you would get to a creative book was a pop-up or 'lift the flap' book in the school library?

Despite dire predictions about the demise of the book industry, publishing is still big business – you only need to go into any branch of Waterstones or other large stores to see the shelves bulging with high quality and beautifully produced books.

Yes, we can produce and publish them ourselves now and that's exciting too because it gives *anyone* with value, expertise, experience and information to share, an outlet for their work.

With the advent of eBooks, audio books and self-publishing in general, comes additional creativity in the content that we can put out, and one great idea that is growing in popularity is the 'Diary of a…' book.

Here, you literally write a diary and then publish it when you reach a natural end point. I know of two people who are doing this right now.

An acquaintance of mine has for many years been a sales and marketing consultant, but he's always had a hankering to be a commercial airline pilot.

Then, one day sixteen months ago he announced to his friends on Facebook that he was taking the plunge and starting his training. It's been fascinating to watch his posts as he reaches milestones along the way – passing of exams, solo flights, first night flight etc.

But he told me that he has also been documenting the journey 'on paper' and plans to publish his personal journey through flight school and all the way up to the day he takes command of his first commercial flight.

He told me that there have been many 'ups and downs' (excuse the pun), and that it could be a valuable resource to anyone else who wants to either start a career as a pilot – or for people who would like to consider a career change, but who don't necessarily think they could do it successfully.

I know someone else who used to be a financial adviser, and after stopping work to raise a family decided to move into education.

She joined a secondary school as a Teaching Assistant and subsequently got a great role as the school's full-time Careers Lead. It's a big role, and apart from anything else requires new qualifications to be attained.

But she too is writing a daily diary of what it's like to be a Careers Lead, what's involved in the role, the challenges faced by school budget cuts and everything she learns along the way - in the hope that her 'warts and all' book will help others who are considering such a role.

Her book will not only be of interest to those who are considering a career in Careers, but also to teachers and others in schools potentially all around the world.

She's doing it purely *because she can*. Before self-publishing came along, such a book would be unlikely to ever see the light of day. But now, she can finish her 'diary book', format it for Kindle and/or paperback, upload to

Amazon, create a cover using their online tool, set a price and that's it.

If she uploads a version for paperback, Amazon will give it an ISBN number and print it on demand for anyone who wants to buy a copy. Her royalty payments will be visible in her own Amazon dashboard which are then paid out to her bank account.

It is literally that easy!

What about IFAs and Financial Advisers?

Only this morning I had a Zoom call with a regional manager for a large firm of financial advisers. We were finalising a presentation I was going to give at their forthcoming conference, and she was telling me that as a firm they are increasing looking for more and more resources to support new entrants to the profession.

They already give them support with exams and qualifications, but they were also looking for help with personal development, business development, marketing and so on.

Not only that, looking at the posts in our LifeTalk group on Facebook, there are increasing numbers of questions from young or new financial advisers who are also asking for advice and pointers on personal development, business development, marketing and a wide range of related topics.

If I was starting out as a new financial adviser right now, I would love to have access to book or resource from a more experienced adviser – and a book, eBook or audio book called 'Diary of a Financial Planner' would be ideal.

Granted, *Diary of a Financial Planner* might not be the snappiest or sexiest of titles, but you get my drift…

How hard could it be for an IFA, financial planner, life planner, wealth manager or mortgage adviser to spend just five to ten minutes a day for six months or a year writing their diary?

You could start that *today*. And who knows, when you publish it, you could be potentially helping someone to take that first step into this great profession…

Co-Authored Books

There are of course many permutations on the book theme, whether an eBook, audio book, published or self-published book.

We've already touched upon the interview format, but another approach is to co-author a book – perhaps with another expert in your field.

The benefits of co-authoring a book include:

- Less time needed on your part

- Another person or persons to promote the book

- Working with other people can bring additional strengths to the project

- The opportunity to bounce ideas off each other

- Quality over quantity – rather than stretch out your ideas, focus on just the highest quality content

- You become accountable to someone else

As we heard earlier, Martin Bamford of Informed Choice Independent Financial Planning, co-authored *Ready, Steady, Retire!* with Justin King of MFP Wealth Management.

Why don't you team up with another financial adviser and put together your own book?

Multi Author Books

Multi author books are also popular where you write just one of the chapters, but at the very least you have a product that you can give away or sell in a variety of settings.

From time to time, there are co-authoring opportunities with big names in the speaking and consulting world.

For example, *Driven* (Celebrity Press) is a book featuring one of the world's leading motivational speakers and authors Brian Tracy - and nineteen other authors.

One of the other authors is my friend Georgi Gunchev who is highly successful in the insurance world in Bulgaria.

Each person contributes their own chapter based around a particular topic and has the opportunity to be included on customised versions of the cover with Brian. Here they are together on the cover of the book.

PHILIP CALVERT

Clearly this gives Georgi a fantastic promotional opportunity and platform to promote his own services.

These are also known as 'anthology books', and of course when you are included in a book alongside someone like Brian Tracy, you are all but guaranteed to be part of a worldwide best-seller.

Other authors who have headed up such books include Jack Canfield, Larry King and Dan Kennedy.

In many ways I'm quite surprised that more financial advisers have not grouped together to create a multi author book. It would be an exciting project to see come together and because each adviser only needs to write one chapter, it would not take too long to create.

And in this time when the financial advice profession needs to work harder at promoting the value of its services, such a book would be a powerful way to represent itself positively to consumers.

The book need not even be for profit, with any monies made being donated to charity.

Mini-Books

We talked about Tips Booklets earlier, which are at the very low end of the market – really simple, thin pocket-sized guides which fit easily in a pocket or handbag.

Although they may be at the low end of the market, they are still perceived to be valuable and have sold well over many years.

Now let's take it up a notch or two and create something which is still a book containing tips, but which is presented more professionally.

Mini-Books are just that – physically small compared to a traditional paperback and no larger than around 17cms by 12cms. They will typically have fifty to ninety pages, but will have good, if not high production values and therefore something to be proud of.

Examples of these are the 'Authority Guide' series which cover everything from Mindfulness, Conflict Resolution and Financial Forecasting through to Public Speaking, PR for Small Businesses, Performance Management and more.

From the financial advice world, Michelle Hoskin's *Best Practice Makes Perfect* is a great example, and in 86 pages contains 171 tips for advisers. Michelle has also co-authored a second mini book called *The Little Book of Woww!*

Mini-Books can be either published or self-published, the latter being the case for both Michelle's books. If going down the self-published route, yes, it's quick and easy to get your product out there, but if you want it to sell, make sure that you have a market for it.

Special Reports and White Papers

Another form of writing which can be published or self-published is the Special Report or White Paper. That said, they can also be downloadable PDF files.

Special Reports and White Papers tend to be A4 sized documents which are much more detailed and academic in tone and which address a specific problem or issue.

They can also be education pieces which highlight a new development or perspective on a topic.

Often, they will be high quality, factual and authoritative analysis of research into a topic and can therefore command high prices – often into the thousands of pounds.

Pensions, investments and retirement planning can be complex, and whilst the financial advice profession is working hard to make it clear and attractive to people, there is very much a place for more in-depth information, and these topics are very well suited to the Special Report or White Paper market.

For example, perhaps you specialise in employee benefits – it is likely that there will be local companies who would find your writing of value and be willing to pay for your research, analysis and expertise.

For financial advisers, regular publication of White Papers or Special Reports is a great way to differentiate you from others, and as a result can be valuable in enhancing brand image and awareness.

Typically, you would sell your report on your website or a dedicated page but could just as easily be sold at the back of the room after your seminar or through advertising in HR or other specialist publications.

In addition to the profits that selling your reports can create, 'White Paper Marketing' is a powerful strategy in its own right. Yes, it can be time-consuming, but exponents often remark on the high quality of leads that they can generate.

An important side benefit of writing Special Reports and White Papers is that they can often lead to lucrative consultancy work.

Courses

I often think that financial advisers are missing a big trick when it comes to how they sell their expertise and experience.

We've already looked at several new ways, including seminars, webinars, books, eBooks and so on, but the fact is that the way consumers access financial advice has barely changed in over fifty years. Hopefully with this book we are beginning to see that technology is our friend and can help us to not only deliver financial information in a variety of new ways, but also to make money from it.

And there's the clue – financial information which people can choose to act upon in their own way. The simple fact is, there are millions of people out there who need the help and advice of a financial adviser, but don't actually want to go and visit one. Sorry, but that's just the way it is.

And that view is perpetuated by the fact that we have the internet, which is only too willing to help us find what we're looking for.

Nevertheless, people do actually need and want your help, even if they don't want to come and see you (yet).

Talk to any doctor these days and they'll tell you how many patients turn up for their appointment with a sheaf of papers under their arm which they have printed off Google. Self-diagnosis is rife today, but most doctors don't see this as a problem – in fact many see it as good because thanks to the internet, people are now empowered to take control over their health.

True, incorrect self-diagnosis can be dangerous, but doctors will tell you that for day to day minor ailments, most of the time the patient has got it about right, but they still go to see the medical practitioner for the all-important prescription.

We will increasingly see this in financial advice and wider financial planning, with people using internet and technology to self-diagnose, but still needing the advice of an expert (that's you) to implement the most appropriate plan.

Even cashflow modelling will soon be a regular occurrence through mobile apps, with challenger banks having a big role in this.

The opportunity for financial advisers is to become part of the solution after people self-diagnose their financial situation, and this can be done in a variety of ways – seminars, webinars, eBooks etc. as we have already mentioned.

But what about other solutions?

Pete Matthew of Jacksons Wealth Management in Cornwall already provides the education piece through his popular podcast (over 2.5 million downloads) but is now experimenting with online courses through his financial education brand MeaningfulMoney and the MeaningfulAcademy.

Clearly all the information in his blog, podcast and videos is generic, but he is fulfilling a valuable financial education role which leads to new client enquiries, including three separate ten-day email courses.

Using free financial education as a lead magnet is extremely powerful, but can just as easily be charged for, and this is the real opportunity for financial advisers who are looking outside the box.

Your course could be delivered in one or more of a variety of formats:

- Email
- Recorded video
- Live video (Zoom, Skype etc.)
- Audio
- Video and Audio
- Tele classes
- Webinars
- Monthly live classroom trainings at a venue
- Live one to one training
- Membership sites (more on this to follow)
- Via an App
- eGuides
- Audio PowerPoints
- Hard copy workbooks
- Facebook Lives in private groups
- Augmented and virtual reality

Clearly there is a lot of choice in the way your education is presented and the delivery mechanism. You can also employ gamification techniques to enhance the experience and help ensure people complete their learning.

To summarise the benefits to financial advisers of creating their own courses:

- New ways for consumers to find you and be educated by you

- Brand awareness

- Differentiation from other financial advisers

- Build community amongst people who take your courses

- An additional income stream

- Enhances the perception of your authority and expertise

- Licensing and white-label opportunities

Membership sites and Communities

Hosting your course inside an online group or membership site is a simple and popular option, largely because the available software for creating online communities often includes built-in features to host modular courses – ClickFunnels and Mighty Networks being good examples.

A quick Google search will help you find others, and bear in mind that Facebook and LinkedIn groups are also a good basic model you could use to build your community. Indeed, many Facebook and LinkedIn groups have tens of thousands of members and have formed the basis for building very robust businesses around a chargeable membership model.

The chargeable membership model is a powerful and proven business idea, helping you to have that all-important recurring revenue stream.

To learn more on this I highly recommend the excellent book *The Automatic Customer* by John Warrillow. See https://amzn.to/2KJGpkY

There are also membership communities for people who run membership communities! Again, Mighty Networks has a group called Mighty Hosts, whilst there are others such as TRIBE and The Membership Guys. They all provide excellent information on building your online community, including the pros, cons and best practice on charging for membership.

Whilst I've spoken a lot about the importance of writing your own book, I'm increasingly of the view that speakers, consultants, financial advisers – anyone who could sell information – should have their own membership community. And there are distinct benefits of doing so:

- Build community around you, your brand and expertise

- Communicate instantly with potentially thousands of people

- People will join who won't necessarily become one-to-one clients, but who will purchase your information products and services

- Members become advocates and will refer you. Many will become 'raving fans'

- Listen to what your members are interested in and serve them accordingly

- A more reliable, stable income stream

- High potential for upsells and additional profits

- Your content positions you as an expert, if not *the* expert on a particular topic

- Membership growth can be exponential with no additional overheads or costs to you

- It need not be location dependent, but can still offer local 'real' events

A private membership has in itself, perceived value, because being part of a group of likeminded people is a core benefit of membership communities, particularly when you have a common goal.

People also aspire to be part of such communities, as they have the effect of elevating status – again, particularly when there is a learning goal attached.

I currently run three online membership communities, with two others in the pipeline:

1. **LifeTalk** for IFAs and financial advisers, with groups on Facebook, LinkedIn and Mighty Networks

2. **SpeakerCom** for professional speakers, coaches and consultants on LinkedIn and Mighty Networks

3. **LinkedIn Marketing Secrets** – for anyone who wants better and faster results using LinkedIn in their work or business.

My SpeakerCom group on LinkedIn currently has 24,500 members but I am in the process of moving the group over to Mighty Networks because the functionality for community development is so much better than on LinkedIn.

LinkedIn Marketing Secrets started life as a Facebook group, but again I am moving it over to Mighty Networks and will then close/archive the Facebook group.

I am in the process of creating a niche group for financial advisers, around the theme of this book, so IFAs/advisers can network, share best practice, exchange ideas, help each other – and so on.

Whilst Facebook and LinkedIn groups are free to run and which can grow very large in a short period of time, there are some serious shortcomings worth keeping in mind:

- The content you see on LinkedIn and Facebook is controlled by algorithms – even in groups. This essentially means that the algorithm tells your members what to see and they often miss the content that you actually want them to see.

- Facebook may be fun, but it is far from conducive to focused networking and there are multiple distractions.

- Facebook actively promotes competitors' groups to your members.

- Both LinkedIn and Facebook are predominantly advertising platforms, which distract from the content in groups. It's also inevitable that Facebook will begin running ads within groups at some point.

Add to that concerns about privacy, data breaches, hate speech, conflict, misinformation, politics etc., I for one would rather use a platform such as Mighty Networks which is both advertisement and algorithm free and has a much more professional feel. They are also specifically designed so that hosts can charge for membership, private groups and courses.

Whilst one of the main benefits of having a membership site is the ability to have potentially thousands of members - size, of course, isn't everything.

Yes, the ability to promote and sell information products to thousands of people is exciting, but a small and high-quality network can be just as valuable and gives you the host, the opportunity to give far greater attention to individual members.

Many membership sites are built round very tight niches, so value is much more important than size. Take these examples of the power of niche communities:

- The Brothers Brick – a community for leading LEGO builders.

    Andrew Becraft founded The Brothers Brick in 2006 to spotlight awesome builds and techniques as well as interview the leading lights of LEGO building. The site now boasts a thriving community of over 300,000 on Facebook.

- Goats of Anarchy – a community for people who care for goats with special needs

- Young Chefs Academy – courses helping kids build both their skills and their palate

- Girls Auto Clinic – helping women to get comfortable repairing and caring for their vehicles

- The Car Seat Lady – videos, guides and installation lessons for growing young families

- The Sourdough School – help, courses and recipes for baking sourdough

- Compton Cowboys – men from the inner city who ride through the streets of LA on rescued horses acting as role models for kids

- The Minimalists – helping people pare down their possessions, and live a healthier more intentional lifestyle

And four for financial advisers:

The Financial Diet

In their own words: "It's really hard to talk about money. Chelsea Fagin does it for you on her website and 595,000-subscriber YouTube channel. Her tag line is "the luxury of spending less," and she's found massive success helping people save more money and enjoy the things they do buy."

Curtis "Wall Street" Carroll - Self-Taught Financial Redemption

"Behind bars in San Quentin serving a 54-to-life sentence, Curtis Carroll knew he had to turn his life around. So he taught himself to read and then started a financial literacy program for other inmates. His 2017 TED talk, "How I Learned to Read – And Trade Stocks – In Prison" has been viewed over four million times."

The Retirement Answer Man - Relatable Financial Podcast

"We all dream about the moment we can step away from the workforce and into retirement, but Roger Whitney knows not everybody is financially ready. His breezy, engaging podcast has attracted a big listener base of people preparing to quit their day jobs without having to worry about what comes next."

As mentioned earlier - Jared Reynolds - partner in Wilkerson & Reynolds, an advisory firm in Columbia who specialises in working with Bass fishermen.

Jared has grown his business by forming a niche working with Bass fishermen, where he arranges fishing and hunting trips, and so gets to spend hours or even days at a time in close proximity with small business owners to form relationships.

For any financial adviser, it is well worth listening to Michael Kitces' interview with Jared as it gives fantastic insights into the value of working in a niche and how it can be expanded. Check out the Financial Advisor Success podcast interview at www.kitces.com/blog/jared-reynolds-wilkerson-bass-fisherman-niche-passion-prospecting/

I should also draw your attention to Certified Financial Planner Jeff Rose, from Nashville, whose eight-year-old YouTube channel boasts over 425 videos and 272,000+ subscribers.

Whilst Jeff is a financial planner, the focus of his videos is on 'life and wealth hacks', where he shares fantastic content on ideas around making money that you were never taught at school. His style is energetic and fun, and his videos are packed with useful information.

His playlists cover:

- Interviews with entrepreneurs who have created passive income streams
- Easy wealth building strategies
- Wealth hack Wednesdays
- Online business success hacks
- How to invest and make money

- Life productivity hacks

www.youtube.com/user/goodfinancialcents

Whatever your community or niche, the communication and content delivery mechanism is almost irrelevant – it's the community that counts, whether it's based round Instagram, YouTube, a Facebook group, Podcast or a dedicated membership site.

Either way, your membership site/community is another fantastic addition to your Value Ladder, and I would highly recommend you consider building one. You can make it chargeable or keep it free but use it as a high value lead magnet for your bespoke financial planning and advice services.

Look after your Community

However, please don't underestimate how important it is to keep your members engaged – because when you crack this, you have something incredibly valuable for you and your community.

If you are thinking of getting started with your own community, here are some tips to keep in mind:

Firstly, I highly recommend that you join any community which supports community builders, because invariably you will discover a wealth of valuable expertise, tips and help based on practical experiences.

As mentioned earlier, Mighty Hosts is excellent at https://hosts.mn.co

Second, don't stress or give up if you are adding content to your group but hardly anyone is joining. Keep at it – the people will come!

Third, ensure your group or community has an overall theme and goal. Professional community builders call this your *Big Purpose* – your motivation and challenge for your group. It's a phrase coined by Mighty Networks founder Gina Bianchini.

The best Big Purposes for online communities are:

- Specific - You can picture clearly the end state and how each of us in the group will be better for taking on your particular 'quest' or joining your movement.

- Exciting - It's going to be fun and challenging every step of the way.

- Easier Achieved Together - It won't be easy, but if we work together, it's possible.

You can see straight away that online communities work best when members are encouraged to share stories and experiences that everyone else can benefit from. They are less about giving people advice, and more about sharing how people have tackled issues and moved forward.

Within our LifeTalk groups for financial advisers on Facebook and LinkedIn, it's clear to see that the best and most engaging content is when members are first and foremost sharing their stories and experiences. The proof of how valuable this is, is the amazing number of financial advisers who have written to me over the years saying that they have made major business decisions based on the *stories and experiences* of others within the group.

As the group host, what's noticeable is that as soon as a thread tips over into giving advice to one another on a particular course of action, the conversation starts to slow down and often hits a dead end.

One of the characteristics of social media is that people are incredibly quick to share advice, and all too often that becomes overwhelming when dozens or more people pitch into a topic with their advice too.

It's great that people are willing to share advice, but as a community host it's important to set the scene when people join, that what members value more is your experiences. They can then draw their own conclusions and make their own decisions as to what course of action to take on a particular issue they are facing.

By way of an example, this is the Big Purpose we have written for our online community for professional speakers:

Within SpeakerCom, we're defining together what it takes to be a great speaker; to build an exciting, profitable and compelling speaking business and to attract more of the speaking opportunities that we really want in 2019.

Within the SpeakerCom community, our goal is for every member to gain confidence and make progress towards achieving their speaking goals – through sharing of stories, best practice, failures and successes in a safe and friendly environment.

> *No ads, no algorithms, no negativity or distractions – just support, encouragement, community – and fun!*

Other tactics to employ in your community include:

- Icebreaker questions – the first thing people see when they join. E.g. *"What do you hope to get from a community of your peers?"*

- Member interviews and stories

- Polls and surveys

- Occasional provocative questions – and I stress *occasional*!

- Monthly themes with relevant weekly content

- Goals for the week

- Share challenges you might have

- 'Wednesday Wins'

- Content organised within topics

- Online and 'real' events

- Weekly summary of the most engaging content over the previous seven days

Regardless of the topic or theme of your online community, there are also lots of fun things you can do to engage members which always go down well, such as:

- On Fridays ask members to tell you about their week in Just Three Words

- Post a picture taken during the week

- Post a picture of your pet

- Describe what you're best at in two words

- Tech Tuesdays – favourite apps and software

- What is your favourite album of all time?

- Fuck Up Fridays! Tell us about something that has gone wrong this week.

  Yes, I have seen this one being used, and despite the language, it always gets a good response. Depending on who you are targeting with your community, clearly this one is optional!

You might think that asking people to post a picture of their pet in a professional forum is a bit trivial. But as part of your overall content strategy, occasional use of posts like this work very well. Often you will see huge numbers of your members taking part.

Questions are a great way to engage your community. I have seen all of these used to good effect:

- Where did your talents come from – luck, hard work or your genes?
- Which person outside of your family has had the most influence on your life?

- What is a project you are planning, but just can't get started?
- What was the career you never had?
- Which personal development books have really changed you?
- What are your favourite podcasts?
- What is one thing you want to improve this week?
- How would you describe your brand?
- What are you currently procrastinating about in your business?
- What do you want to be held accountable for this week?

I have dozens more questions like this – please drop me a line for a list if you would find it useful.

I'd love you to join either **LinkedIn Marketing Secrets** or **SpeakerCom** and be part of *my* community. You can find them at https://linkedin-marketing-secrets.mn.co and https://speaking-professionals.mn.co/

If nothing else, take a look at the landing pages to see how they have been set out and presented to potential members.

Networking Groups and Meetings

Of course, your community doesn't have to be based online...

There are many financial advisers who still swear by face-to-face networking meetings as a full-proof way to attract new clients.

There are many local and national networking groups around the world, so whether your clients are based in the South West of England, Dubai or Northern Ireland – there will be a networking group for you. Your local Chamber of Commerce may well have regular meetings and is a great place to start.

BNI (Business Network International) is the world's leading business networking and referral organisation, and I know many financial advisers who are regular attendees.

But if BNI is not your thing, then just Google 'Networking events in...' and you will soon find something. One of my personal favourites in the UK is NRG Networks and you can find them at www.nrg-networks.com/

Just like generating referrals, there is a skill to networking. Many financial advisers are content to rely on clients referring them to other people, but if you take the trouble to learn the art and science of building a networking and referral strategy, then magic happens, and the quality of your referrals increases significantly.

Networking is the same. Simply turning up to an event with some business cards won't be enough to make networking truly effective. There's a skill to it and it's well worth your time learning how to be a great networker.

Networking expert Andy Lopata has written some great books on the subject and it's well worth checking him out.

As well as Networking to attract Clients, how could you use Networking to create a valuable new Income Stream?

Whilst I've had many financial advisers tell me that they love BNI, I've had equally as many tell me that it's not for them – but they do still enjoy networking and attending networking meetings. In fact, some have developed quite impressive 'elevator pitches' that they have crafted over the years.

An option for those of you who are interested in networking but who don't enjoy the BNI-type experience, is to set up your own networking club. I've seen various people do this in a variety of industries and it works along these lines:

- Find a local venue such as an hotel, pub or something a bit different – as long as it has catering, or at the very least a bar.

- Create an extra page on your own website or build a simple one-page site which promotes your new local networking club. The emphasis is on local.

- Contact local businesses of all sizes, saying something like:

> *"Many local businesses wish that there were more networking opportunities in [Town/Village], so I'm setting up an informal networking club.*
>
> *We're meeting on the first Thursday of every month at 5pm in the back room of The Dog and Duck. I'd love you to join us for a drink, informal networking and a short presentation from me [or a local speaker].*
>
> *Your first meeting is free – and please bring a friend because everyone is welcome. Don't forget to bring your business cards..."* etc.

- People can register on your website or by email, text etc.

- At the meeting, welcome people and keep it relaxed and friendly. Introduce your speaker (which could be you or a local business owner) and conclude with more networking and drinks from the bar.

- Close by inviting people to come along next month. Entrance fee will be £10 (or whatever) and encourage them to bring a friend. First timers are free.

I admit that this does sound quite a laid-back approach, but it works.

You can always make it a bit more formal as the membership grows, but in the early stages keep it relaxed. Clearly as your group grows, you'll need to think about venues, and you might need some admin support and branding but stick to this simple model and it works well.

If you use a funnel type landing page, you can automate the whole sign-up process – complete with reminder emails and SMS messages.

You could even use a private Facebook group to set up the whole thing and use the built-in events tool. LinkedIn is also relaunching its events tool, so you could also use that for sign ups etc.

And for the avoidance of doubt, you do not have to restrict membership to one person per profession; the idea is to build a networking group which coalesces around its members, you and your business.

And this is the point, you are once again looking to build community around you and your brand and create something which people want to be a part of. If you have written a book, you are perceived to be an expert – if not the expert on a topic. Writing a White Paper or Special Report does the same thing – and hosting your own networking events also positions you as a person of value and influence in your local community.

The world's first B2B social networking site was called Ecademy. Whilst it was based online, the founders still ran local networking events around the UK, and the model I've described is exactly how Ecademy got started.

In London alone, after starting with just half a dozen members meeting in a bar, monthly attendance ended up in the hundreds and created an amazing sense of community.

For many small businesses in the early 2000s, Ecademy was the making of them with the powerful blend of online and offline social networking.

Whilst Ecademy was formed in 1998, LinkedIn wasn't launched until 2003 – but it is only now that you can attend LinkedIn networking meetings. Even these meetings are not official LinkedIn events, and are run by enthusiastic members who value meeting the real face behind the profile.

Whilst there are Terms and Conditions to running a LinkedIn Local event (a bit like running your own TEDx event), in theory any member can set up a group – so this is another option if you are considering creating your own networking group or series of meetings.

Clearly not everyone who attends your meetings will be your ideal client, nor will you necessarily want them to be - and that's fine.

This approach is very much aimed at financial advisers who include businesses, business owners and executives within their client mix - but who like the idea of using their brand and their business to create something of value in the local community and which can bring in a new income stream alongside their traditional financial advice services.

And it goes without saying that attendees of your networking events will then do your marketing for you, as they refer people to not only your networking meetings but hopefully also to your financial advice business.

Do not underestimate the importance of *networking and networking opportunities* as a powerful draw to your business. Perhaps businesses and businesspeople are not your target market and that your focus is on retired or near retirement folk; but if you are hosting a seminar or client appreciation event, you should always state in your promotional materials that it is "…a great networking opportunity".

Humans are social animals and are naturally drawn to events and places where they know that there are others just like them, so use networking as a marketing tactic regardless of who you are targeting with your services.

Executive Mastermind Groups

Let's now look at a product/service that you can offer which is a hybrid of events and seminars, private memberships, community building and networking.

Right now, Mastermind Groups are all the rage amongst coaches and consultants, yet they are not new. Wikipedia describes a Mastermind Group as follows:

"A Mastermind Group is a peer-to-peer mentoring concept used to help members solve their problems with input and advice from the other group members. The concept was coined in 1925 by author Napoleon Hill in his book *The Law of Success*, and described in more detail in his 1937 book, *Think and Grow Rich*. In his books, Hill discussed the idea of the Master Mind, which referred to two or more people coming together in harmony to solve problems."

In short, putting several minds together to discuss a problem often yields solutions that far outweigh what anyone could have come up with on their own. But it's not just the solving of problems where Mastermind Groups come into their own.

Benefits of joining a Mastermind Group:

- Support through community
- Accountability
- Talk through problems
- Help to achieve goals
- Develop new skills
- Collaboration

- Help to think bigger
- New perspectives on business issues
- Tap into the skills and experience of others
- Find and share inspiration
- Tap into little-known resources
- Brainstorming ideas
- Grow your network
- Additional opinions on your own ideas
- Get help to finish projects you've started
- And much more

So from a personal and business point of view, there are many advantages of joining a Mastermind Group, and everyone I've met who has been a member of one says they are incredibly valuable.

In addition to the benefits of joining such a group, financial advisers also have the option of speaking at groups and this is usually for a fee.

In addition to smaller, independent Mastermind Groups, there are also larger ones run by organisations such as MD2MD and Vistage (now incorporating the Academy for Chief Executives). These two tend to focus on CEOs but there are many other peer-to-peer business groups looking for speakers.

In the UK, look out too for Midlands Leadership Groups, the Academy for Business Leaders, Executive Foundation, the Yorkshire Leadership Group and several other local organisations.

From my own experience of speaking at such groups, the format tends to be similar around the world, with the speaker joining the meeting during the morning and speaking up to and sometimes including lunch, so you're presenting for two to three hours. Not only do you meet some fascinating people from great businesses, but if you do a good job of your presentation, then you often get more business working either one to one with attendees or being invited to run an inhouse workshop with their team.

Out of a room of about twenty people, you could easily be invited to work with five of them over the coming weeks. And even if you don't get invited to work directly with an attendee's company, you can also get referrals to businesses outside membership of the group. Not all Mastermind Groups have as many as twenty people, with up to ten being most common.

Your presentations at such groups are more of a workshop than a keynote type offering. Attendees want to get real value which they can take away and apply in their own businesses, and the value, expertise and experience provided by a financial planner would work well in this environment.

But another option for financial advisers is to start their own Mastermind or peer-to-peer business group. I won't go into the format here because there is plenty of advice to be found in books and on Google. Suffice to say that hosting your own Mastermind Group is an extension of the networking idea mentioned earlier, where you build a community around your brand. That community has profound benefits to its members, whilst also creating income and leads for you.

You can start from scratch or start your own Vistage group, but do also bear in mind that the financial side of things is not the be all and end all of running your own group. You can just as easily create a small group where the sole focus is on supporting each other. What's more, you don't even need to meet in the flesh, with Skype and Zoom being other options to meet.

In summary, your options are:

- Join a Mastermind or peer-to-peer business group
- Speak at Mastermind Groups
- Create your own non-profit Mastermind Group
- Create your own for-profit Mastermind Group

Each has its own distinct benefits for financial advisers, but either way consider choosing one option.

Run your own Conference or Online Summit

The thought of putting on your own conference may sound somewhat daunting. Clearly if you're planning anything with more than two hundred delegates, it is – not to mention a large financial commitment/risk.

However, it need not be as daunting a task as you might imagine, particularly if you keep it small and beautifully proportioned.

At the risk of mentioning Martin Bamford again, he did just this. Not in his capacity as a financial adviser, but in his role with Bamford Media – a small marketing agency in Cranleigh, Surrey.

Martin called the event The Financial Planner Marketing Summit and invited ten marketing speakers from across the profession to speak to an audience of financial advisers. He booked a small theatre venue in Guildford, kept it simple and with the minimum of fuss, and it was a great success.

Clearly it was a promotional event for his marketing agency, but I admired the simplicity of the approach, and it was proof that putting on something like a conference is easily achievable with careful thought and planning.

There is no reason at all why any financial adviser couldn't take the seminar model I described earlier, and scale it up to something larger – complete with a range of external speakers. Once again, such an event will create valuable publicity for your business, whilst positioning your firm as a provider of high value to the local community.

But perhaps a conference is not for you…

How about trying something along the same lines, but completely online.

The Online Summit

Early in 2019 I tried an experiment which turned out to be one of the most exciting and enjoyable business projects I've ever undertaken.

During the previous year I had taken part in a couple of online summits – one as an attendee and the other as a speaker, where I was interviewed over Zoom for 'The Infopreneur Summit'.

This was a week-long online conference/summit for people who create information products – just like those described in this book.

In total there were fifty-two speakers, all of whom were interviewed by the summit host Bailey Richert. Over the course of a week, Bailey released approximately ten video interviews per day, and each video was live for just twenty-four hours.

It was free to watch the videos, but if you upgraded to the 'All-Access Pass', you could have lifetime/unlimited access to the videos, plus a wealth of additional bonus materials in a private membership area.

This was broadly the model that I used in my experiment – *The Financial Adviser Mastermind &*

Challenge, which featured over thirty leading financial advisers and industry consultants.

Taking part were:

- Brett Davidson
- Jacqui Harper MBE
- Abraham Okusanya
- Michelle Hoskin
- Martin Bamford
- Rohit Talwar
- Carl Richards
- Ian McKenna
- George Kinder
- Tina Weeks
- Michael Kitces
- Jason Butler
- Chris Brindley MBE
- Pete Matthew
- Roger Edwards
- Thorsten Jekel
- Julian Treasure
- Phil Young
- Frank Furness
- Penny Haslam
- Justin King
- Bill Cates
- Dr Lynda Shaw
- Colin Lowe
- Derek Borthwick
- Catherine Morgan
- Michael Dodd
- Clive Waller
- Richard Emery

…and Kriss Akabusi MBE. So some heavy hitters!

In short, it worked a treat. Here's how:

Over six hundred IFAs and financial advisers registered – that's six hundred who received massive value from the content – and who consented to join my email list. Many of whom were not members of my LifeTalk groups on LinkedIn or Facebook and have gone on to join them.

Fifty percent upgraded to the All Access Pass where they could get unlimited access to the videos, plus MP3 recordings and multiple other training videos for advisers.

The event was the first of its kind for financial advisers in the UK and received rave reviews from the IFA community.

Providers have subsequently asked if they could be part of the next Financial Adviser Mastermind & Challenge, with some saying they would like to sponsor it.

Three large financial adviser firms have asked for white-labelled versions of the summit so that their advisers can have permanent access.

We have subsequently added even more video trainings and interviews and now promote it as a permanent online training resource for advisers.

Other benefits that have come out of hosting the summit include:

- I have built relationships with 32 industry influencers in the UK and overseas

- I've been asked to appear in several industry podcasts as a result of hosting the summit

- I now have a source of valuable content which can be repackaged into a variety of other products (e.g. a book of the entire event)

- I've received multiple testimonials

- I have been referred to other paid speaking work

- I have tested a model which works, and which can easily be applied to a variety of other industries

Why not run your own Summit…?

OK, so it's easy for me to say host your own summit, but clearly some work goes into it. Not least of which is that you will need to come up with a target audience, a theme, invite speakers/interviewees and then record interviews with them.

You'll also need a platform or membership tool to host the videos plus a site to promote the event, but there are a number of proprietary tools to make it easy for you.

I fully expected this to be incredibly labour intensive, but once I had put together a spreadsheet listing everyone who I would like to interview, it came together very quickly. I came up with a list of eighty people I wanted to invite and then sent emails to fifty of them, keeping the remainder in reserve.

Out of fifty emails to advisers, experts and consultants in the UK, US, South Africa and New Zealand, only one person declined. Almost everyone was thrilled to have been invited and willingly took part. Each speaker got a copy of their video, with many of them mailing it to their client list and using it in their own marketing materials.

The interview process turned out to be much easier than I was expecting, with Zoom being the ideal tool to use because a) it's easy to connect with people anywhere around the world, and b) the system automatically records the conversation.

I kept the interview style relaxed and conversational and almost without exception focussed questions around:

- How did you get started?
- What do you know now that you wish you knew when you started out?
- What are the characteristics of the most successful financial advisers?
- What challenges do you see coming up for financial advisers?
- Spin-off questions that came up from their answers

At the end of the interviews, I asked each person to set a simple challenge that financial advisers watching could take up and implement in their business over the coming days, weeks, months etc. Advisers with the All-Access Pass could then join a private online forum where they could talk about the challenges, ask questions, get accountability partners and report back on their progress.

The challenge aspect is not normally included in the online summit model, but I included it because I felt it would be valuable to viewers as a way to encourage them to act on the content they had listened to.

Would I do it again?

Yes, definitely and I plan to integrate it into one of my membership sites. I will be doing it again for financial advisers and am also putting one together for coaches and consultants.

What about you?

As a vehicle for differentiating your financial advice firm, adding value to existing clients and creating an income stream, I would highly recommend putting together your own summit.

As mentioned above, think of it as a conference with multiple speakers, but online. Unlike my own summit with over thirty speakers, you could easily do it with a dozen to get you started. The point is that you are putting something together which is extremely high value for the benefit of your clients or local community.

On which Topics could a Financial Adviser run a Summit?

In the financial planning space, you could have expert speakers on:

- Investing
- Retirement planning

- Later life planning
- Equity Release
- Long term care

Equally you could run a summit which focuses on:

- Health and wellbeing
- Personal development
- Retirement lifestyle
- Etc.

Another option could be to run a local business summit where the speakers are all from local companies. This is on my To Do list and potentially something of high value to the local community – perhaps in partnership with the local Chamber of Commerce. In this case the summit could be completely free, with revenue coming from advertising. Another option could be that businesses would pay to take part in the interviews.

Obviously, there are many ways to do it and monetise it, and we're only limited by our own imaginations as to which route to take. The point is that summits are a proven model and could be a great opportunity for financial advisers looking for a new revenue stream.

If you have not joined the Financial Adviser Mastermind & Challenge, you can get your access at www.adviserlifetalk.com/adviser-fast-track

Software and Apps

Another way for financial advisers to broaden their interests is to create their own software. Like putting on your own conference, at first glance this might seem like one option too far!

However, over the years in my online forums for financial advisers I have often seen members suggesting ideas for simple software tools that would help them in their businesses, but they don't know anything about coding and have no idea where to start.

They also have the perception that it will cost hundreds of thousands to produce and will take many years of development.

But things have changed...

Firstly, let's go back in time to the early 1990s. I was a broker consultant working with Zurich Life in the City of London. On my patch was a financial adviser business called Quay Securities run by Roland Rawicz-Szczerbo – today the owner of Time4Advice.

Roland agreed to meet me to hear about our new Critical Illness products, but while I was there, he showed me how Quay was measuring the profitability of their client bank. He opened up a spreadsheet of data on his clients, which turned out to be the first version of the popular IFA back office software Client Care Desktop (CCD). CCD was eventually run by Quay Software which later became part of Capita.

The point...

Often financial advisers have ideas for systemising a common process in their office – or indeed in their industry, and if it can be systemised it can be turned into software. Another thing you can do is to create your own spin on a tool or software that already exists.

Thanks to the internet we can now get our ideas turned into working software, quickly and easily – and without it breaking the bank. There are even software tools that will help you to generate ideas and to get your project off the ground.

One resource you might want to look at is Software Secrets. You get a book, a web class and access to software that gets you started. In the interests of full disclosure, I have not got the book myself, neither have I tried their process, but I know several people who speak highly of it. You never know, it could work for you.

Get your copy of Software Secrets free at https://softwaresecrets.com/free-ss-book

Another way to engage your audience and potentially create a new income stream is by creating your own mobile app. If you have come up with a software idea, the chances are it could also work as an app.

But maybe you have come up with an idea for a *standalone* app…

Once again, you would be forgiven for thinking that this will take a huge budget and specialist skills. Well it could, but another option is to build it yourself!

No idea how to code an app?

No problem; try DIY sites like appmakr, Bubble, Appie Pie or Odoo. Or, go to Fiverr.com and find a freelancer.

Now, you won't be able to build your own version of Facebook, but you'll be able to create something that you will be proud of and have it available to millions of people around the world through the iOS and Android platforms.

The first step is, as usual, to think about where your app sits on your Value Ladder. Is it something that you give to people for free or will it be chargeable to use? Or, free but which takes advertisements.

Most of the DIY app making tools give you a free trial, so one idea is to sign up for a trial and then just play around with the drag and drop functionality that most of them have. After you have tinkered with it and can see what is possible, ideas will start to come to you.

As we speak, I'm working on a simple app, and just playing with the DIY tools' options, has given me some exciting ideas to move the project forward.

More Ideas

So, there we have twenty-three different ways to monetise your expertise, skills and experience as a financial adviser, but there are of course permutations on the theme which I've listed out below.

Again, use your imagination as to how you could take what you know and repackage it into a variety of information products that will have appeal to not only your existing clients, but also those who need your help but in a format that better suits them.

1. Field guides
2. Study guides
3. Survey and research tools
4. Template packs
5. Audio quick takes
6. Video documentary
7. Video subscription series
8. On-demand video mini-lessons
9. 12-36 month consulting packages
10. 3-12 month coaching programs
11. Action Packs
12. Implementation Kits
13. Assessments
14. Toolkits
15. Card decks
16. Beginners Guides
17. Manuals
18. Handbooks
19. Laminated quick reference guides
20. Personality profiles
21. Games
22. Online quizzes

23. Mentor programs
24. Audio PowerPoints
25. Checklists
26. Worksheets
27. Reminder cards
28. Posters
29. Flipbooks
30. Masterclasses
31. Transcripts
32. Certification programs
33. Training that can be white labelled and licensed to others
34. Translations of any of your materials for use in other countries

Do any of these catch your eye? Let me know and we can brainstorm how you could use them in your business.

Your Value Ladder Revisited

Earlier on I talked about your Value Ladder – the route by which we encourage people to engage with us, build relationships and trust and move towards working with us at the highest level.

Unfortunately, most financial advisers (certainly in the UK) have no Value Ladder at all, and it's important that we start to embrace this concept. Here's why…

Pre the internet, when we were looking for a financial adviser, we either used Yellow Pages, wandered into the local insurance brokerage in our high street or possibly asked a friend for a recommendation.

What also happened, was that when the topic of pensions or mortgages came up at a dinner party, our host or someone around the table would suggest their adviser – and we would write down their name and phone number on a paper napkin or the back of our cheque book. The next day we would call them up.

Today it's different.

We're at the dinner party, and when the topic of pensions or investments comes up, our host or someone around the table will, once again, suggest their adviser – and we will jot down their name and website on our mobile phone.

The next day - we *don't* phone them up.

What we do today is look up their website, and while we're about it we run a quick Google search for 'financial advisers in Reading' or wherever.

And because most financial advisers now have reasonably good-looking websites that appear in local search results, we'll take a peek at what they have to say for themselves.

I've done this exercise with my eighty-something mother-in-law when she was looking for a local IFA, and what shocked me was that all seven of the sites we looked at, said exactly the same thing.

Other than their logos, there was very little to differentiate them and nothing that could help us choose one over another. The only possible way to do that was to phone up each and every one and get a sense for how well they engage with us.

In our online forums for financial advisers, they are constantly asking about how to generate leads, yet my own research suggests that most of them have more than enough leads right under their noses.

Where are these leads?

They are visitors to your website who left without looking at a second or third page and we failed to capture their attention.

Let me explain…

Over the last twelve months I've been looking at adviser websites. I've been doing this because the question of websites and lead generation is being asked more than ever before by advisers. And working with my IFA coaching clients I've noticed something quite shocking.

Several things are happening – or *not* happening as the case may be...

Firstly, over the Summer of 2018 I gave multiple presentations to groups of IFAs around the UK. In September alone I presented to about a thousand financial advisers, which is a good sample to use.

These advisers included small, 'boutique' type firms, traditional IFA and adviser firms, CFPs and Chartered Financial Planners. In short, a good mix.

When I asked for a show of hands to the question *"Who knows how many website visitors they've had over the last week, month, sixth months (whatever)?"*, hardly anyone put up their hand. Over the final three presentations to approximately three hundred advisers, no-one put up their hand at all.

This amazed me and compares starkly to presentations that I give in other industries and professions – including automotive, law, accountancy, tourism, interior design and independent opticians, where practitioners have a noticeably better grasp on their website numbers.

This means that financial advisers would seem to have little or no idea at all about what's happening on their websites.

They don't know:

- How many visitors they've had over a given period
- How many pages of their site were looked at

- Which were the most popular pages on their site
- How long visitors stayed on the site
- What search terms they used to find them
- The location of site visitors
- And most importantly what the 'bounce rate' is. We'll come on to that one...

When I ask those same advisers if they can tell me how many cases their professional introducers have referred, or how many client referrals they have had over a given period, they can give me a pretty accurate picture without looking it up – but clients that had come via their website are a complete unknown.

Now there is a LOT of data that Google Analytics and other packages can provide you, much of which is not needed by most financial advisers - but the absolute basics that you need to know are the ones I've listed above. Even if you don't get the numbers yourself, someone in your firm should get them for you because it is key management information in the digital age. These are numbers that you *need* to know.

Once you know this information and have tracked it over a period of weeks, you'll be able to see trends and make changes that can improve your numbers.

I work with a number of financial advisers on monthly Skype/Zoom marketing coaching calls, and without exception each has been staggered at their website stats when presented to them. But they are equally amazed at how easy it is to improve the situation with a few simple tweaks.

And improvement is what you will inevitably see when you know your numbers and react accordingly.

What's going wrong with advisers' websites?

Close examination of advisers' website numbers reveals clues as to why they are far less effective at converting visitors than they should be. And ultimately it comes down to the amount of value and interaction that the site offers, and the quality of the copy.

Ironically, most adviser websites provide *too much* value, or put another way, the wrong type of value.

Let me clarify.

Over the Summer we looked at one hundred adviser websites at random. Most 'looked' reasonable enough with the usual themes, but a clear pattern emerged immediately when we dug deeper.

Firstly, when we counted up all the clickable links on their home pages, the average came out as thirty-four. That's thirty-four clickable links on the home page alone. That's thirty-four potential calls to action.

Now, personal finance and financial planning can, for a lot of people be complicated and confusing enough as it is, without arriving on a financial adviser's website to be faced with thirty-four places that you can click.

Yes, your social media buttons count as clickable links too - as do the Contact Us, About Us, Blog, News, Fees pages and all the others.

The problem stems from a few years ago when financial advisers and other businesses were first getting started with websites.

Back in the day, the emphasis was on making your website home page 'sticky', and the idea was that you put as much information as possible on there, in an attempt to a) hold people on the page and b) get picked up in Google search results.

Back then, that was exactly the right thing to do, because websites for financial advisers were still a new idea, and by putting on loads of content you had a new medium with which to highlight your expertise and your services. The content would then be picked up by Google and you would appear higher in search results. The mantra we used to teach advisers was *"If you're not on Google, you don't exist."*

And if you were appearing in Google search results, that was a big differentiator from other financial advice firms.

Today, if we have a home page with multiple links, all we end up doing is confusing people and making them hesitate. And when it comes to websites, a confused mind will always say No and your visitor will leave. If you want people to make enquiries, you MUST keep things simple and highly relevant.

If you want to get picked up by Google, don't just cram the home page with content and links. Instead consider:

- Having a fast-loading, mobile-friendly website

- Having a fast-loading, desktop site

  Not sure if your site is loading quickly enough? Check your speed issue at https://developers.google.com/speed/pagespeed/insights to learn what you need to do to speed things up

- Work on your keyword strategy – use tools like https://neilpatel.com/ubersuggest

- But don't overdo keywords – make your copy readable by humans

- Add your most important keyword(s) to the title of content on your pages and also early in the copy on each page

- Claim your physical address on Google Maps

- Create a blog and add regular and consistent **high-quality** content

- Promote your blog content on Social Media

- Reach out to influencers in your field or niche and ask them to share your content

- Build a network of friends and contacts who are willing to share your content on Social Media

- Use Google Analytics or similar to monitor the performance of your site

- Write a unique, keyword optimised title for each page

- Remove anything that slows down your site when loading

- Remove so-called 'Zombie pages'. You need fewer pages, but with higher quality content

- Try to get links to your site (backlinks) from other reputable and relevant sites

- Work harder on optimising your title and description tags to increase clickthrough rate in Google search results. Clickthrough rate is an important factor that Google takes into account when determining where you appear in results

- Optimise any images with relevant keywords

This is just a short list to get you started, but a great resource for information on SEO (Search Engine Optimisation) is anything from Neil Patel. Check out his YouTube channel at www.youtube.com/user/neilvkpatel

In short, the financial advice community is not using its web presence strategically, and our sites are still being seen as an opportunity to put everything we've got out there - all wrapped up in attractive beach scenes and couples wandering hand-in-hand through Summer meadows. It's really no better than standing in a shopping mall handing out leaflets and brochures and then hoping that someone might get in touch.

The great thing about a website is that someone has already arrived, and by definition they have the potential to be a warm lead. They are right there waiting for you to take them by the hand and take them where they want to go.

Unfortunately, our websites generally only serve to confuse visitors and do nothing to guide them in the right direction.

And this takes us to the inevitable second BIG problem…

Because there are so many clickable links on our home page alone, the next important website statistic looms menacingly into sight… The Bounce Rate.

The Bounce Rate is the percentage of your site visitors who arrive on your site (from whatever source) and then leave without looking at a second page.

The higher your Bounce Rate, the worse your site is performing (unless your site only has one page).

The lower your bounce rate, the better. In fact, any financial adviser website with a bounce rate of 20%/25% or lower is doing well, but even then, a quarter of your website visitors are leaving without visiting another page. And the simple reason for this is because there is far too much on your home page – and what there is, doesn't encourage interaction with you.

So we did some more research…

What we discovered was that out of the hundred adviser websites we looked at, the bounce rate averaged 54%. Several had bounce rates of 74% with a few at 80%+. Ouch.

And all the while, the adviser business owners had been pleased with their investment in their shiny website but had no idea how it was performing. In fact, they weren't performing at all and were simply not turning visitors into enquiries.

Turning things around

The exciting news is that this can easily be turned around without you having to spend a fortune on expensive designers.

My personal philosophy is that your website should be doing just ONE of two things - Either, converting new site visitors into enquiries...

Or, adding value to EXISTING clients.

Your site shouldn't try to do both. Our research has shown very clearly that advisers' sites that try to be all things to all people, just end up turning people away and up goes that bounce rate again.

What converts your website visitors is:

1. Having a crystal-clear idea of what your ideal client looks like and providing content that hits them between the eyes

2. Knowing exactly what financial planning issues and problems they are likely to be facing

3. Giving them something of real value on your website that will not only get their attention

immediately, but make them eager to learn more about you

Does that make sense?

The 'something of real value on your website' is a lead magnet, and its job is to:

- Lower people's resistance to engaging with you

- Instantly give them something that gives answers to their problems and issues and which is of real value to them

- Start the process of building a relationship with you

- Adding them to the foot of your Value Ladder

- Giving you their contact details

For most financial advisers, the humble eGuide or a PDF Tips Booklet will be sufficient, but many of the products we've talked about in this book could just as easily do the job.

But ideally, whatever your lead magnet is, it should be directed at the primary need of your ideal client.

So if as an adviser your niche is (say) heart surgeons, you will know exactly what the main financial issues and problems are that are faced by heart surgeons, and your lead magnet should be presented as something that:

1. Proves you know and understand their problems and issues

2. Slightly agitates their concern and makes them eager to get an answer

3. Provides instant value and information on that subject.

Heart surgeons won't necessarily have the time to implement the solutions in your lead magnet, but your downloadable guide will at the very least get them into your funnel.

This is just one example, but what I hope you can see is that your expertise, skills and experience as a financial adviser has value that goes far beyond sitting face-to-face with a client. It is value that can be used to attract clients and value that can be sold to clients in a multitude of different formats.

Example Value Ladder

We looked at Tony Robbins' value ladder earlier, now let's look at another so that you can apply the same principle to your own business.

Here's the Value Ladder that works for many dentists (Source: ClickFunnels):

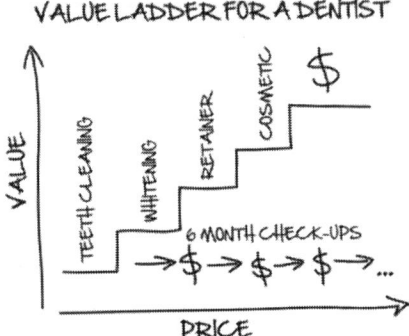

As you can see, they are using **free Teeth Cleaning** as their Lead Magnet, and some dentists will even periodically offer free Teeth Whitening as their bait. If not free, they will offer/upsell the whitening at the time of doing the free cleaning.

What's more the dentist him or herself doesn't even need to do these treatments themselves! And what they will also do is give them great customer service and even get a video testimonial there and then.

Here are some thoughts on items that a financial adviser could include in their Value Ladder:

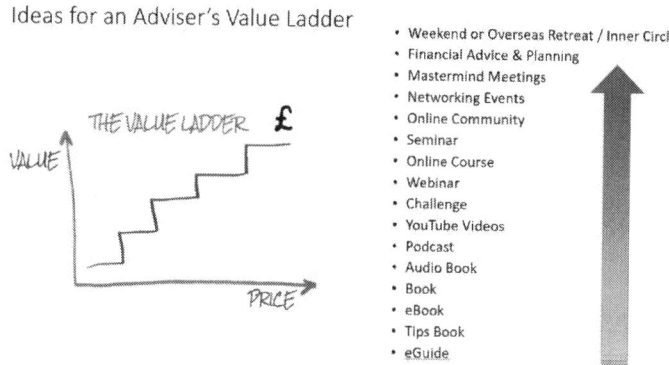

As you can see, we have talked about every item on this list in this book, and they range from the eGuide at the bottom, right up to the Weekend Retreat.

Each has their part to play in attracting new clients and adding value to existing clients. Most financial advisers aren't going to offer anything like all of these products and services, so you should choose those that you feel comfortable with and which you feel will offer most value.

Typical Value Ladders or 'Funnels' for a financial adviser might look like this:

eGuide > Webinar > Seminar > Financial Planning

Or perhaps:

eBook > YouTube videos > Online course

Or maybe:

eGuide > Podcast > Financial Planning

Or:

Seminar > Tips Booklet > Financial Planning

Or:

Seminar > Online Community > Mastermind Group membership

Or:

eBook > Online Course > Inner Circle

Or:

Podcast > Webinar > Financial Planning

Or:

eBook > Webinar > Financial Planning > Mastermind Group membership > Weekend Retreat

Or:

Webinar > Online Course > Weekend retreat

Or:

Book > Mastermind Group membership > Financial Planning

As you can see, the permutations are endless, but construct a Value Ladder that works best for *your* business and the types of clients you are trying to attract. The Value Ladder you create for a heart surgeon will clearly be different from one you create for a first-time house buyer.

It's fair to suggest that most financial advisers will construct a Value Ladder or Funnel which ultimately leads them to a financial planning consultation.

But it's also worth bearing in mind that it's entirely possible to have a strategy where you never have any personal contact at all with the client, with the entire Funnel being automated. Hence meeting the needs of people who need/want your help but want it on their terms.

This raises the question of how we define the word 'Client'...

Is a client *only* someone to whom you provide your usual financial planning (face-to-face or over Skype/Zoom) services? Or should 'client' also include someone who has given you their email address in exchange for your eGuide?

It's entirely possible that you may never meet the person who downloads your humble eGuide, but in time they could become your most valuable client through the purchase of your other products and services.

For many people, the first time they ever come across Tony Robbins is via his free videos on YouTube. They may then go on to download his book – and later attend some of his events.

This same person could, in time join his Platinum Partnership programme, so we should never underestimate the potential lifetime value of all clients – regardless of how they come into our business.

Going up a Gear

If you really want to take this stuff seriously, there is no reason why you can't create *several* Value Ladders, each of which with its own separate website or funnel that is custom designed for the job.

There are a variety of software tools that can do this, my favourite of which is ClickFunnels. ClickFunnels provides ready-made templates, automated email follow ups and mechanisms to take credit card payments. It's an all-in-one solution.

Get a free trial using my link at http://bit.ly/Philfreetrial2019

Once you get more advanced, you can start offering upsells when people purchase something, and this is where the real money is.

The purpose of this book is to alert you to what is possible from your expertise, experience and skills, but typically an upsell will be where someone downloads your free eGuide or eBook, but you also offer them the Audio version for a modest price while they are still 'warm' and excited.

And just like the eGuide itself, they get instant access to the audio file. A variation on this theme is that you send them a pre-loaded MP3 player in the post, and simply because they get the audio version on a physical product enhances its perceived value.

As Russell Brunson points out in his fantastic marketing book *Dot Com Secrets*, McDonald's make only a tiny profit on its sale of a burger to you; but when they then upsell you fries and a drink, they make eight times the profit of the original sale.

With our Financial Adviser Mastermind & Challenge, we offered the entire thirty video training for free. But many people also opted for the upsell, which was unlimited access to the videos and multiple additional trainings and resources. Although they could watch all the videos for free, people still opted to pay £97 because they could see obvious value.

This is the point behind having a Value Ladder – people can build a relationship and trust with you through your free value, which then makes it much more likely that they will progress the relationship further.

Your Challenge

If you've read this far, I'm reasonably confident that you can see merit in taking your knowledge, expertise and experience and repackaging it in some way, shape or form.

For many financial advisers, what I'm proposing will be seen as a fundamental shift in how they do business, and that will feel uncomfortable because as I mentioned earlier, the way financial advice professionals work with clients has barely changed at all in decades. Yes, technology has impacted how we run our businesses, but the way we work with clients is still based on the face to face model – albeit some of that interaction is now done over Skype or Zoom.

But in the work I've done with IFA clients over the years, most can see some merit in broadening their horizons a little. And what has been fascinating is that with some thought and brainstorming, it's quite easy for them to come up with something simple to get them off the ground.

A hurdle for some is their perception of what Compliance will say, and that's fair enough. Compliance are there to do a job. But when you work *with* Compliance, you'll be surprised at what they will allow and what you can achieve.

When I was Head of National Accounts for Zurich Life, I was looking for novel ways to get our Broker Consultant team in front of IFAs around the UK. We had some great products, but the challenge was persuading advisers to spare valuable time to meet with our boys and girls on the road.

I came up with the idea of running eight full day workshops for IFAs around the UK and Northern Ireland, where we didn't once mention our products, but spent the whole day talking about marketing ideas for financial adviser businesses.

When I put my idea to the executive management team, they shot it down in an instant saying things like:

"What a waste of time – we need to get our products in front of IFAs, not fluffy marketing nonsense"

"We won't be able to measure ROI"

"What if your marketing ideas don't work and advisers sue us?"

"Who knows what you'll say in the presentations - Compliance will never allow it"

What I hadn't mentioned at the start of my presentation to the executive team, was that I had already spent time sitting down for a friendly chat with Compliance to get their feel for the idea.

I had explained to the Head of Compliance what I was trying to do, which included:

- Give IFAs something they are constantly asking for – sales and marketing ideas for their businesses; not just our products

- Positioning Zurich Life as not just a provider of products but also of added value

- Differentiate ourselves from every other provider out there

I also compared the cost of a Broker Consultant meeting with advisers one-to-one, day in and day out, with the cost of eight one-to-many presentations around the UK. One-to-many won hands down.

To cut a long story short, Compliance were fine with my idea. They asked for a copy of my presentation for the workshops and that was about it. I reassured the executive team that Compliance were indeed happy, and the project was given the sign off.

I was able to report back three months later that we had managed to get a full house at each location – that being 150 advisers at each of eight separate venues. What's more, the advisers had loved it, and meetings between our Broker Consultants and attending advisers had increased by 80% in the three-month period immediately afterwards.

I repeated the same approach when I was with Permanent Insurance and got the exact same results.

The point though is that when we are so used to going about our business in a particular way, we often immediately discount another way of doing things, citing an easy reason why it can't happen.

I agree that there are far too many Compliance people at larger financial advice firms who are making it hard for their advisers to try new things. Many of these Compliance people still regard Social Media as a 'new thing', and make it very difficult for advisers to effectively make use of Twitter, Facebook, YouTube etc.

So things do need to change at these firms, but advisers could be doing a lot more to help themselves, by taking the approach I have outlined and talk to Compliance one-to-one, highlighting what you are trying to achieve and the benefits that can come out of it.

When you can show them that your (say) eGuide is not making any financial promotions, not giving financial advice and not potentially bringing the company into disrepute, providing it includes any necessary risk, regulatory and other wordings they would like included, you can usually work with them to reach your desired result.

Compliance people do not like surprises, so if you foresee problems with anything I have talked about in this book, sit down and talk to them *before* you do anything. The simple fact is that there is nothing that I have suggested in this book that can't be created or achieved by a financial adviser.

Next steps

So what will be your next steps? Sit back and say, *"It's not for me"*?

Maybe think there's something in this but worry you won't be able to find the time to do anything?

Agree you could definitely do something, but never get around to it?

Start jotting down ideas right away?

Here's just one reason why you should choose the latter:

A little earlier I mentioned Nashville based financial planner Jeff Rose. In one of his YouTube videos he interviews a man named Jeff Goins.

Jeff Goins was earning $37,000 per year as a marketing director for a non-profit organisation but ended up quitting his job after he wrote his first self-published PDF eBook about Blogging – earning him $150,000 *in just six months*.

It had no ISBN number and started out for sale at $2.99 on a simple and cheap eCommerce website (E-junkie).

Jeff kept the price deliberately low because he was afraid that no one would buy it, but in the first 48 hours, a massive five hundred people purchased it. In his eBook's first weekend, he made $1,500.

After a few weeks, sales started to slow down, and after taking advice from another eBook author who had made $40,000 in two months from her own $4.99 eBook, Jeff changed the title, reworked the content a little and moved it to Amazon where he could benefit from the huge distribution opportunities there.

In the first month after his launch on Amazon he made $3,000; then $4,000 in the second month and $5,000 in the third. By the end of the year he had made $50,000 from the book and then turned it into an online course, making an additional $100,000.

The time taken to do all this? Just one month to write his eBook and get it online. He sold ten thousand copies in the six months after launch. Since then, Jeff has gone on to write several other traditional published books and eBooks.

In short, Jeff's quick, easy and cheap eBook changed his life, and all I am suggesting in *this* book is that you consider creating just one product to see what happens.

Jeff says that first eBook actually started life as a PowerPoint presentation. A few weeks earlier he had given a short presentation on blogging to a college journalism class. He said:

"I took the slides from that and added some notes and stuff, and then exported it as a PDF and put it live on E-junkie. I just wanted to create something quickly to see if it would bring in some money. I certainly didn't think I had a business."

Jeff's tips:

- Build your network and email list over time through blogs and other online content

- Communicate regularly with your network/list with free value

- Network in the real world to build relationships and further increase your list and reach

- Ask or survey your network what content and products they would like from you – what would they like to learn and what would they be willing to pay for

- Write your content and publish it on Amazon

- Don't stress about perfection – just create a 'minimum viable product'. Remember, Jeff's eBook was just a PDF document created on his computer

- Ask your network to promote your product

Jeff's example is far from unique, with many people making good amounts of money online with simple information products.

Yes, there is still a very strong market for traditional books, but thanks to technology there is a huge amount of opportunity for anyone who has expertise, experience and knowledge to share.

Having worked with financial advisers for over forty years, I'm excited about the future for face-to-face financial advice, but I'm convinced that there is an amazing new opportunity for delivering financial information and expertise to consumers in new ways.

Within the context of a clear Value Ladder, financial advisers have a wide range of expertise that can be packaged up and delivered to them.

What's the Best Way to get Started?

This book includes many examples of products that you can create quickly and easily. You could even take Jeff Goins' approach and start with a PowerPoint presentation that could be updated and enhanced.

If you haven't got a presentation that you've used previously, PowerPoint is a good place to start laying down your thoughts. The fact that one slide follows another is a helpful way to logically organise your content.

However, before doing anything, I recommend that you start by answering five questions:

1. What is your area of expertise?
2. What problem do you solve?
3. Who specifically do you solve it for?
4. How do you currently solve it?
5. How else could you help to solve it?

This might seem a very simplistic approach, but in any kind of product creation – real or digital, the answer to these questions will guide you as to the route or routes you could follow.

Let's take a closer look with an example…

What is your area of expertise?

I'm an expert in helping business owners to plan their financial futures – particularly in retirement.

What problem do you solve?

I take away the stress and worry of not being properly financially prepared for retirement.

Who specifically do you solve it for?

Owners of small to medium sized technology businesses in Manchester.

How do you currently solve it?

By building close and trusted relationships I work with them to plan their retirement income, and through cashflow modelling I help to ensure that they won't run out of money.

How else could you help to solve it?

Through educational content at seminars in Manchester, which will give them another way to engage with us to get answers to their questions. We could also include a high-quality guide or report on the financial problems and issues typically faced by owners of technology businesses.

Our seminars would also give them the opportunity to network with each other – something that is important to business owners in the technology space.

We could also consider creating a dedicated monthly networking group for owners of technology businesses in Manchester as a next logical step.

In answering these five questions, the adviser now has a clearer focus on how his or her expertise can be repackaged and sold to their target market in the most appropriate way. A seminar might normally be used as a lead generation exercise, but in this case, it is a product in its own right. (And clearly, it could also double as a lead generation exercise to attract new clients in the Manchester area.)

So, your Value Ladder for this particular target market might look something like this:

Free Seminar and Report > Financial Planning > Chargeable Networking Group membership

It could also look like this:

Financial Planning > Free or Chargeable Seminar and Report > Chargeable Networking Group membership

Or this:

Chargeable Seminar and Report

In the case of the latter, your event and report is a product/service in its own right, which will have appeal to a certain group of business owners in the area, who perhaps already have a financial planner or who are just interested in what your event and report have to offer – or indeed who are looking for a second opinion on their current planning.

Yes, in time attendees at this event may become financial planning clients, but not right now. At the very least, you have made some money from them, and with permission, they are now on your mailing list. They may well also refer you to others.

There are no hard and fast rules as to how your Value Ladder is organised, though as we've mentioned previously it will typically go from:

Free or Low Price > Mid Price > High Price and High Value

Ideally, you are looking to create a ladder where the value of your products and services progressively increases in price – or which is specifically designed for a group of people in a niche.

My advice is to play around with different ways that you can solve your target market's problems and find something that works for them and you. Answer the five questions for your own business and see what comes up.

Progressing the Relationship

In the previous example of technology business owners in Manchester, you could also have decided that an eGuide could warrant a place on your Value Ladder as a really simple way to attract attention and leads to your financial planning services.

Perhaps you are already known in the Manchester area as an expert on financial planning for technology businesses, and your website already reflects that in its design, content, keywords and perhaps advertising on Google.

It's likely too that there will be owners of very small start-up technology businesses in the Manchester area, who whilst not yet in a position to even think about retirement planning, might show at least some interest in a few pointers that they should be considering as the years go by and their business grows.

These people are not on your radar as potential clients because they don't fall within your traditional target market. However, you are still in a position to serve them with some value, and possibly to the extent that they will pay for products and services that are more relevant to them.

If your website, PR and wider marketing reflects your specialism, it is likely that these people will at some point find your online presence. When they do, here is your opportunity to start building a relationship with them through a simple and free eGuide download that meets their needs or solves their problems.

Not sure what information they would find valuable?

Ask them! That's one of the things Jeff Goins did.

But here's something really important to remember if you are offering eGuides as free downloads and lead magnets on your website...

Just because they exchanged their email address for your piece of, albeit relevant value – it does not necessarily mean that they have a relationship with you. That's something you have to work at.

There is a difference between someone who has opted in for something and someone who is a lead for one of your services. If you are cold selling pest control products door to door, and someone answers your knock at the door – are they a lead?

Of course not. It will take some dialogue and good old-fashioned sales banter to take place before they could even remotely be classed as a lead.

It's the same online. Just because they download your free eGuide, they are not necessarily a lead for something else – but we are in the right territory.

If they can see that your eGuide is high quality and has real value to them, then it makes it easier to progress the relationship further.

For that to happen, you need to have thought about your next move – hence the need for having a Value Ladder, so that you have a logical next step for them to take. So in the case of the younger technology entrepreneur your Value Ladder might be:

eGuide > Podcast > Webinar

Or:

eGuide > Webinar > Chargeable Seminar

Or:

eGuide > Free Seminar > Facebook or LinkedIn group membership > Chargeable Online Course

Once again, you can see that there are no hard and fast rules, other than a logical series of steps that age and ascend the relationship between you.

In this case, you are able to serve people who are *similar* to your ideal target market, but who are not there yet. And you've done this by taking what you know and repackaging it in a way that suits this other market. You also make money along the way.

Building the Relationship Further

Having thought about what the next logical step is for them on your Value Ladder, we need to help them to get there, and we do that initially through email.

There is currently a trend towards using Bot communications to build relationships, particularly on Facebook, but email is still considered to be the best way to engage with people who have downloaded something from your website.

When someone first requests your download, a couple of things can happen:

First, they enter their email address and are taken to a second page where they find their download.

Or, they are taken to a second page where there is a *thank you* message and possibly an upsell. They say yes or no to the upsell and are either directed to the download page or sent the product separately by email.

Most experienced internet marketers will take your visitor to an upsell page, because that is where the real profits are (see the McDonald's example earlier). In this case it could be that the initial download is free, but they are subsequently offered the audio version for a modest fee.

Some marketers will offer a real physical book as their lead magnet on the basis that it is free, but you pay a few dollars/pounds for the shipping. Even having to pay $5 or so for the shipping will be sufficient to eliminate most timewasters.

So they get their book for free; they pay for the shipping and while they still have their credit card out, they are then offered an upsell of the MP3 audio version of the book for anything up to $20 or more. I've seen people charging up to $100 for the audio version of a free book and depending on the design of the upsell page and how the offer is presented, the take-up rate for the audio version can be surprisingly high.

Some online funnels like this will offer multiple upsells and even down sells, and again, if done well the take-up rates can be excellent. But let's not run before we can walk.

But if you don't offer an upsell, you need to make sure that they get your download quickly.

If being sent separately by email, this can all be automated, using a variety of proprietary tools such as:

- ClickFunnels
- HubSpot
- AWeber
- MailChimp
- ConvertKit
- Constant Contact
- Etc.

However, it can also be done manually, and when you first start out this is the easiest option (and cheapest).

When you send out your eGuide or download, this is not the time to go into sales mode for the next product on your Value Ladder. However, if your next step is free membership of your Facebook or LinkedIn group, it is perfectly OK to highlight this. In fact, offering something else of value which is free can work well. I've been doing this for years.

In your accompanying email you could say something like:

Hi Sue...

Many thanks for visiting our website today and for your interest in our eGuide – I hope you'll find it useful.

Many people who download this guide also join our private Facebook group, where you can meet others like yourself, network, ask questions and share ideas and experiences around running small technology businesses.

Members often tell us how useful the group is, and you can join us here [Link]

Thanks in advance...

Bill Jones

Nice and simple and not salesy at all. Every IFA or financial adviser who I connect with on LinkedIn is sent a similar message suggesting that they might like to join my Facebook or LinkedIn groups for advisers, and most take it up.

From there you will be able to see if they go on to join your group. If they do, you could then restrict most of your subsequent communications to go through your group. If you are a member of a Facebook group, you know how it works, with Facebook doing the messaging leg work for you.

If they don't join your Facebook or LinkedIn group (or maybe you don't have one), you then have the option of building the relationship through email communications.

As an important side point here, for GDPR purposes you need to ensure that when they enter their email address on your download page, that you include a consent message and tick box for them to agree to receive further emails from you.

Quite apart from being for GDPR purposes, the act of asking people to consent is good business practice and will help them to build trust in you. You should also state that their email address will remain private and that you won't spam them or pass on their email to anyone else.

So to recap briefly, Sue has visited your website and has claimed her free eGuide or download from you. You have delivered her guide and she may or may not have gone on to join your private Facebook or LinkedIn group if you were offering membership, and she may or may not have been offered an upsell in the process.

If the next step on your Value Ladder is (say) a free webinar, if she has found your eGuide useful, then clearly Sue may be more inclined to take notice of your subsequent promotions for your webinar.

But in an ideal world we don't want to start promoting it at all. Not yet, anyway.

The first step is to, through email (or posts in your group), give Sue additional free and relevant value. This will be through short tips - written as experiences, case studies or stories.

Your emails need only be three or four paragraphs long but should focus on giving Sue valuable information that could help her in her business. Clearly it might have a financial theme to it, though need not. Either way, the content will be information that you know is valuable to people in her position.

Your first email will be sent to Sue the day after she receives her initial free download. It should have no sales message at all and should only focus on building on the eGuide with additional tips.

For example, if your initial free guide promised *'20 Proven Tips for Small Technology Businesses to XYZ'*, then your first follow up email could include Bonus Tip Number 21.

On day two of your follow up emails, you could give Sue Bonus Tip Number 22 – and so on for seven days. Some marketers follow up the initial download over eleven days.

Even seven days of follow up emails may seem like a lot, but when done well – i.e. they include clear value and absolutely no sales pitch for anything else, most recipients will be fine with it.

In your first follow up email, you should set expectations for Sue and state that this is the first of 'Seven Valuable Bonus Tips which she will receive over the coming week'. That way you have given her the heads up that she can expect a message each day. You might also want to ask her to whitelist your email address so that they don't go straight to her spam or junk folders.

You should also ensure that the follow up emails go out at the same time each day, so the recipients come to expect them in their inbox. Naturally each email should fully comply with appropriate standards and law and give the recipients the opportunity to opt out of receiving further communications, and clearly you should respect the decision of anyone who does this.

On receipt of their final email, then and only then should you highlight your forthcoming webinar – or whatever is next on your Value Ladder.

The webinar itself does not have to be broadcast on Day 8, but you have at least alerted them to the fact that it is coming up at some point and that they may wish to pre-register.

Video Email Sequences

As an alternative way to follow up someone who has exchanged their email address for your download, instead of sending them traditional email, you should also consider video email.

There are very clear benefits to sending video email instead of text email, as highlighted by one of the market leaders BombBomb:

- You are leveraging your greatest asset in your email – you!
- Deeper connection through better communication
- Video email helps to build trust in you
- Video emails are hard to ignore
- Video email is more human and conversational in style
- 81% of users report getting more replies
- 56% report getting more referrals
- 68% report getting more leads when using video email

You don't even need to read the reasons why to know that video email is just far more likely to engage with our audiences. In fact, it won't just help you in your eCommerce efforts, but will be a major benefit in your financial advice business too.

You can learn more about BombBomb at https://bombbomb.com

Another tool that many internet marketers love is Bonjoro, which is very similar. Take a look at www.bonjoro.com

Automation is your Friend

It goes without saying that all of these follow up communications can be fully automated within the systems I mentioned earlier – including the video email tools. This means that you only need to write or record the seven emails once, with the autoresponder tools taking over from there.

What happens is that when Sue enters her email address to request your download, it goes onto a list, with the autoresponder tools firing off the emails each day to her at the appointed time.

Yes, you can do all of this by hand in the early days while you are getting started, but when you get to the point where you are getting more than one or two downloads per day, you will want to automate it all.

If you are offering a webinar in the coming days or weeks, that too can be pre-recorded, with your website, email or funnel software showing it automatically to people as they move through and along your system.

So it's entirely possible to have several thousand people visiting your website and downloading your free guide all on different days, with the email and webinar software doing all of the work behind the scenes without any intervention from you at any point.

Know your Numbers

It is however a good idea to monitor your stats, which may reveal for example that people are opting out of your daily emails on (say) Day Four. If people opt to stop receiving your emails on Day Four, then clearly there's a problem with the contents of the Day Four email.

Maybe it's too long. Maybe it doesn't resonate with the reader or perhaps it's poorly written – we won't actually know unless someone tells us.

You should then create a different email for that day in the sequence and 'split test' it against the original Day Four email. Again, the email automation software will do this for you, and you can then look to see if fewer people are subsequently bailing out on Day Four.

If you see an improvement in your stats with more people now moving through to Day Five's emails, then you can delete the original Day Four email because the new version is clearly more engaging.

You should split test other emails in the sequence if you can see that one or more of them are causing people to unsubscribe, until you have a complete sequence of seven emails which reach most people.

While you're about it, you should really also split test the home page of your website or the page where you offer your free download.

If for example two hundred people are visiting your website every day, but only one person is asking for the free eGuide, then there's a good chance that the page or the offer needs rethinking.

It might also be that your wider marketing is attracting the wrong type of people to your site, but on the assumption that the people you aimed the guide at are visiting your website, then something needs tweaking.

I currently have just this problem with one of my offers. I have no shortage of visitors to the site, but not enough are biting – so something is wrong somewhere.

There could be a number of issues:

- The look, feel and design of your site sucks

- The offer you are making doesn't resonate with your site visitors

- The title of your free guide isn't clear enough about what the reader will get from it or how they will benefit

- Visitors can't see what problem of theirs you are addressing

- Your copywriting isn't strong enough (Hint: It's very often this one)

- There could be a technical issue – slow loading page or maybe the email registration isn't working

Whatever the issue, you need to get to the bottom of it, and the best way to start doing that is to split test the whole page.

Again, if you are using specialist funnel software like ClickFunnels, Kajabi, Infusionsoft, Leadpages etc., most will give you the option to build a second or third version of your home page, each of which is served/shown to your visitors in turn.

Then you simply look at your visitor stats for each of the pages, and note which ones are getting the most sign ups. If one is getting many more conversions than the others, then you can probably switch off the poorly performing ones.

There is no ideal percentage conversion rate for these home pages, because everyone is offering something different and within different markets, so you need to find the page which performs best for you and go with that. Even then, you may still be able to improve on its conversion rate with additional split testing.

If you have the time and resource, you should always be split testing because unless you are getting a one hundred percent conversion rate, you can always make improvements.

Even if you read this book and decide that offering lead magnets and downloads is not for you, I would still highly recommend that you split test the home page of your website.

In the book *108 Proven Split Test Winners*, the author Russell Brunson shared some amazing results that were achieved by making simple tweaks to websites. Here are just a few examples:

- How changing the design of a website, but keeping the same text resulted in a 230% increase in conversions

- How changing the position of the testimonials increased conversions by 101%

- How adding one tiny thing to their blog resulted in them earning $276 for every thousand visitors

- A small down-sell on the order form which resulted in a 614% increase in sales from four times as many customers

- How adding one small additional item for free resulted in an instant 55% increase in sales

- Two magic words next to the order button which increased conversions by 27%

- How removing 20 specific items off a web page resulted in an increase in conversions of 21%

- How changing the colour of an order button increased conversions by 34%

- A tiny tweak to a headline which increased conversions by 58%

- How changing the colour of a headline resulted in a 313% increase in conversions

- How the addition of one word increased conversions by 206%

- And many more examples

In short, split testing your email communications, your website and your offer pages is vital if you want to improve your chances of creating an income stream through any of the means we have discussed.

Building and Strengthening Relationships through Online Groups

You'll recall a little earlier that we talked about offering membership of a Facebook or LinkedIn group as a free but valuable part of your Value Ladder.

We've also talked about the power of Community, but it's worth exploring how your group can in itself, be the home for your entire Value Ladder, and the conduit for growing the relationship between individuals and you.

I would like to use my Facebook group LifeTalk as an example of how this works.

LifeTalk is a group for IFAs, financial planners, advisers, mortgage professionals and other financial advice industry professionals. It has a replica group on LinkedIn with approximately 7,500 members.

At the time of writing, the LifeTalk Facebook group is approaching 2,000 members. But what is amazing about the group is its sense of community, with over 80% of the membership active in some way, shape or form each month. If you are a financial adviser, you may already be a member and so will know the set up there.

I have run online groups for financial advisers in various places since 2004, and from time to time LifeTalk moves to a new home depending on the technology at the time. You would be forgiven for thinking that if we moved an established group to a new website or platform, that this would irritate the members, but on each occasion, almost every member has moved with us. And that's because of the sense of community that we have.

Clearly, if we moved it every year then people would soon get fed up, but our moves have averaged out at once every five years. Our most recent move was from a purpose-built platform to the current Facebook group. Prior to that most financial advisers weren't using Facebook very much, but in the last five years they have all shown up on the platform.

Whilst far from being the ideal home for our financial adviser community, Facebook groups are hugely popular across a wide range of industries. Whatever your niche interest in life, you'll find a welcoming home for you in a Facebook group.

According to one source in 2018, in the past year alone, Facebook Group membership is up 40 percent, with 1.4 billion people - more than half of Facebook's massive user base - now using Groups every month. Of those, 200 million people belong to so-called "meaningful Groups," considered a vital part of users' daily lives.

From hobbies to pets, movies, software and celebrities, you can find people who are just like you and who are keen to share their experiences, ideas and questions.

Businesses too are using the Groups feature more than ever before, some with spectacular success. Indoor cycling workout company Peloton boasts more than 100,000 members in its official closed group, which now registers over 300 posts and 5,000 comments a day.

Even in our closed group for financial advisers of just 2,000 members, it's not uncommon to see some topics being discussed for months on end. As I write, a question about exams started two days ago has already had 114 comments.

Imagine if you could harness Community within your own business...

The first thing to note is that you do not have to have thousands of members for it to be a success – and we'll define 'success' shortly. What is good news is that thousands of people on Facebook ARE interested in content around money and have joined groups to learn more about it.

- The Money Saving Hints, Tips and Ideas group: 293,000 members
- Multiply your Money group: 122 members
- Pete Matthew's Meaningful Money Community: 2,076 members
- Fundamental Investing group: 524 members
- Investing for Beginners group: 7,200 members
- Stock market Trading and Investing group: 8,500 members

* Stats as at August 2019

The list goes on...

Members of these groups may not be your target market for your traditional financial planning services, but they most definitely could be targets for the types of financial education products that we have been talking about in this book.

But it's how you use your group which is where the magic happens.

Simply providing a group for people to join is often benefit enough for members – many describe it as like 'coming home' or 'finding their tribe'. Being in a community (wherever it is hosted) is a powerful and proven draw for people, so make the most of this as a way to attract people to you and your products.

Being able to share experiences is another powerful benefit for individuals, because they feel that by doing that they are contributing to the community.

When you first start your group, it will be quiet – but stick with it and people will join. You can either invite people you already know, or just wait for the Facebook algorithm to do its thing. For example, if someone is a member of one money-related group, Facebook will recommend other money-related groups to them. Or you could promote your group through Facebook advertising.

Link to your group from your website and even put it on your LinkedIn and other Social Media profiles.

But once people are joining, you need to move to the next stage. I call it 'feeding your fish'.

Feeding Your Fish

I liken my group to a fish tank. The Facebook group is the tank, and my members are the fish.

Of course, if you keep fish, you need to feed them. (As I keep telling my daughter).

So, on a Monday morning, I feed my fish. The analogy being that we put content into the group, such as tips, links, questions, resources, ideas etc. Stuff that financial advisers love. Note that we could also send 'the food' in an email to our list, but when posted directly in the group, Facebook's algorithm will alert many members and encourage them to log into the group.

When we feed our fish, they log in, swim around, consume the food, say hello to one another and leave to go about their business.

On Tuesday, we feed our fish again. More tips, more links and more value.

Again, members log in to the group, take a look around, consume the food and then leave for work.

On Wednesday we do the same.

But let's now imagine that on Thursday we forget to feed our fish – what do you suppose happens?

That's right, they still log in, swim around, look for scraps left over from yesterday – and then go to work.

And if we forget to feed them on Friday – they still log in. But just to stretch this analogy, something interesting happens – in that many of the fish will bring their own breakfast, which they share around amongst each other. In other words, they post their own content, ideas and thoughts for the community to enjoy.

Once in a while, we'll give the fish something a little harder to chew on. Instead of fish food, we'll throw a few small stones in the water to create some ripples. And by that I mean we will post content in the group that is a little more controversial.

Sometimes, the topic doesn't even need to be controversial – it can create waves simply by the way it is worded. The example of a post I gave earlier which has 114 comments in two days was one of these – the wording was:

"So, if most advisers aren't passing exams first time... the question is why not?"

It's a perfectly normal question that advisers will happily engage with, but its slightly assertive and pointed tone is enough to encourage more people to get involved.

Had the question been positioned as something like:

"Why do you think it is that many advisers don't pass their exams first time around?"

...it would not have received many more than twenty comments.

Then, once a month, instead of sprinkling fish food into the tank, we'll hurl a brick into the water.

You guessed it – we'll post a topic that is guaranteed to wind up a few people. Yes, we've got a secret list of topics that really wind up IFAs...

Again, it doesn't necessarily have to be something particularly controversial; just the way something is worded or even punctuated will be enough to get high degrees of interaction.

Often, I don't even need to be the person who throws the brick in the water – members will often do it themselves in the way they post something or interact with other people.

The point is, that through our Facebook group we are trying to replicate real life communities, where typically you will find good stuff going on, bad stuff and occasionally very annoying stuff.

If all we ever did was to ensure that our LifeTalk members only ever had the very best, tastiest food to eat – it would eventually become flat. Communities benefit best from light and shade.

So through content which excites, delights and occasionally pushes the membership, we create a community which has been *primed* to be responsive to a wide variety of messaging – including sales messages.

Ascending your Value Ladder from within your Community

Priming is a powerful and proven communication technique which prepares people to positively receive a message before they actually receive it. Recommended resource: Pre-Suasion by Robert Cialdini: https://amzn.to/2MxMnJ5

By posting content in our group on a regular and consistent basis which directly meets the needs of our target market – in this case financial advisers – it makes it considerably more likely that when we do want to include a sales message, they will take it up – often without question.

And this is typically the Value Ladder that we follow within the group with the ultimate goal of selling high value one to one coaching:

Free LifeTalk group Membership > Chargeable but Inexpensive Webinar > Chargeable Live Training Workshop > Conference > One to One Coaching

Does this make sense?

Can you see the logic of taking people along a gradual path of trust and value building, so that it makes it very much easier to take them to the eventual goal of one to one coaching?

If I was to post an offer of one to one coaching direct to group members without any other intermediate products along the way; that, with the best will in the world, would be a tough sell.

In the example above, the Conference step is often missed out, with people requesting coaching immediately after attending a training workshop.

Don't underestimate training as a great product to offer people – whether live in person, or online. And some membership site software is specifically designed to help you offer courses to your members – Mighty Networks and Kajabi for example.

Groups are incredibly powerful as tools to build community around your brand, but also your services. You can also use them to:

- Brainstorm ideas
- Get feedback on products and services

- Run polls
- Build trust by providing value
- Make offers
- Build teams round special projects
- Follow up live events and training
- Create your 'inner circle'

And very importantly, they can create an income stream in their own right when you charge directly for membership.

Final Tips

I hope you have found this book useful and has given you some ideas that you are keen to take forward. Here are a few final thoughts before you get to work.

Firstly, be clear about what you are really good at as a financial adviser, because this will help you to better identify which route you should take in terms of the products you want to create.

The aspect of your business that you are really good at could be a technical skill, a business skill, an interpersonal skill – or also a specialist knowledge of a particular location or target market (surgeons, lawyers, retirees, professional golfers etc.) Think also about other/new ways that you could serve these markets beyond what you already do.

Be specific about who you want to target or serve with your new products. Do you want to create new products as lead magnets for your current services, or are you going to create them to make profits from new-style clients? Or both!

Be clear about your Value Ladder – both in your current Financial Planning business and for the sale of your new products and services.

Keep things simple – depending on your Value Ladder, most financial advisers will find that a short eGuide is a great way to get started. Even if you don't put out the final product, it will give you a trial run and a good feel for what you could do when you really put your mind to it.

And if you don't feel that writing is really for you, consider building a free online community to start with and then build your Value Ladder from there.

One final point…

Everything I have talked about here has been related to your expertise within the world of financial advice and planning. But the chances are you have interests outside work – it could be golf, travel, running, craft beer – something else.

Think about what you know or what you have learnt whilst enjoying those pastimes and consider creating products from your knowledge.

Everyone knows about something! For example, a few years ago I won a major competition for making Gin and Tonics! As a result, I've written an eBook on how you too can make an amazing G&T.

Yes, it really is that easy…

I'd love to know how you get on – or maybe you have some questions or perhaps need personal help to get your product off the ground. Please feel free to contact me at philip@philipcalvert.com where I can give you generic advice or even work with you on your project.

Bonus Tip!

When you have written your book – whether paperback or for Kindle and it's proudly for sale on Amazon, don't forget to ask your readers for a Five Star review! If you have enjoyed *this* book, I would of course be delighted if you could also help me with a Five Star review – it would be very much appreciated – thank you. Please go to http://bit.ly/56Ways

And to say thank you for purchasing this book, you have free access to my private group, where you can get help, advice and feedback on your own product and service creations.

You'll be amongst friends – join us here: http://bit.ly/56WaysGroup

About the Author

Philip Calvert has been working with IFAs, financial planners and advisers for over forty years – both with major providers such as Zurich Life, Permanent Insurance and Pioneer Friendly, and as an independent speaker and consultant.

Phil created the world's first online community for financial advisers and was a pioneer of Social Media in Financial Services.

Today he runs the thriving LifeTalk group for financial advisers and is in demand as a speaker and trainer on social networking and digital marketing within regulated industries.

He has worked with financial advisers in the USA, UK, Ireland, Singapore, South Africa, Netherlands, Germany, Bulgaria and the Czech Republic.

Disclaimer and Terms of Use

This book is provided for research and educational purposes. You do not have resell rights or giveaway rights to any portion of this publication. Only customers that have purchased this publication are authorised to view it. No part of this publication may be transmitted or reproduced in any way without the prior written permission of the author. Violations of this copyright will be enforced in law.

The information services and resources provided in this book are based upon the current internet marketing environment. The techniques presented have been extraordinarily lucrative and rewarding to internet marketers worldwide, however because the internet is constantly changing, the sites and services presented in this book may change, cease or expand with time.

We hope that the skills and knowledge acquired from this book will provide you with the ability to adapt to inevitable internet evolution. However, we cannot be held responsible for changes that may affect the applicability or effectiveness of these techniques.

Any earnings, income statements or other results quoted, are based on our own and the testing of other marketers and are estimates of what we believe you could earn. There is no assurance you will do as well as stated in any examples and could be influenced by a variety of factors, not least of which include work ethic and market conditions. If you rely upon any figures provided, you must accept the entire risk of not doing as well as the information provided.

All product names, logos and artwork mentioned in this book are copyrights of their respective owners. None of the owners have sponsored or endorsed this publication.

While all attempts have been made to verify information provided, the author assumes no responsibility for errors, omissions or contrary interpretation on the subject matter herein. Any perceived slights of people or organisations are unintentional. The purchaser or reader of this publication assumes responsibility for the use of these materials and information.

No guarantees of income are made. The author reserves the right to make changes and assumes no responsibility or liability whatsoever on behalf of any purchaser or reader of these materials.

From time to time, the author has included hyperlinks to external products and services, some of which may be an affiliate link, where the author would receive a commission should the reader make a purchase.

The purchaser and reader assume full responsibility for compliance and compliant use of the material in this book, as defined by their respective regulatory body. No guarantees are made by the author that any of the ideas presented in this book will be acceptable under the purchaser or reader's local compliance regime.

Copyright © Philip Calvert 2019. All Rights Reserved.

Printed in Poland
by Amazon Fulfillment
Poland Sp. z o.o., Wrocław